ALL THE KING'S MEN

ALL
THE
KING'S
MEN

A play by
ROBERT PENN
WARREN

RANDOM HOUSE · NEW YORK

456789B

To Francis Fergusson
and the memory of
Marion Crowne Fergusson

ALL THE KING'S MEN *was presented by Michel Bouché, Arnold M. Brockman and Iris Michaels at the East 74th Street Theatre, New York City, on October 16, 1959, with the following cast:*

(*In order of appearance*)

PROFESSOR	Stan Watt
TINY DUFFY	Roger C. Carmel
WILLIAM LARSEN	Jay Kobler
TOM STARK	Donald Quine
A MAN	Stephen J. Hall
JACK BURDEN	John Ragin
ANNE STANTON	Joan Harvey
LUCY STARK	MaryVan Fleet
DR. ADAM STANTON	Richard Kneeland
JUDGE IRWIN	Alex Reed
SUGAR-BOY	Will Corry
SADIE BURKE	Marian Reardon
WILLIE STARK	Clifton James
MOTHER OF JACK BURDEN	Allyn Monroe
SLADE	Jay Kobler
A SECOND MAN	Stephen J. Hall
FREY	Stephen J. Hall
A THIRD MAN	Stephen J. Hall
THE CROWD	Elizabeth Farley, Edna Jean Lundy, Ralph Mauer, Jay Kobler, Patricia Doyle, Alfred de Graaff

Directed by Mark Schoenberg
Production designed by Gary Smith
Costumes by Sue Spector
Lighting by Jules Fisher
Technical direction by Ivor Balding
Associate producers: Eugene Koblents
Gerald Marks

The action takes place in a state of the deep South.
There are a prologue and three acts.

A NOTE ON PRODUCTION

An open stage is envisaged for this play. No set changes are required, for the story is devised to move by a fluid shifting of light from one playing area to another. Some indication of a structure to the rear—girders perhaps—would be helpful. A low platform is required toward stage center, and a balcony, or small, high platform, a little to either side and back. A permanent group of blocks, one in each of the four main playing areas, may be used for furniture, supplemented, as needed, by simple props. One group of blocks, low and benchlike, is at the center, extreme downstage. One group is at each side of the stage, and one on the platform. Special attention should be given to the creation of mood, and the feeling of locale, through the imaginative use of light and sound effects.

PROLOGUE

At a lectern on the platform, addressing the audience, the
PROFESSOR *appears, a man of early middle age, incisive and some-*
what ironical in manner, with an air of authority. On the plat-
form sit TINY DUFFY, *the Governor, and* WILLIAM LARSEN.

PROFESSOR

Ladies and gentlemen, we are gathered together today to
dedicate this great hospital, which will mean so much to every
citizen of this state—and so much, I may add, to the cause of
science, to which my colleagues and I are humbly dedicated. As
director of this institution, it is my privilege to welcome you all
here, and to welcome our distinguished guests and speakers.
The Honorable Aloysius Duffy, Governor of this state. (TINY,
*overdressed and self-important, rises and bows, with oleaginous
dignity*) And Mr. William Larsen, builder, financier, philan-
thropist. (LARSEN *rises and bows—a gray-faced, quiet, watchful
man, with some trace yet on him of his years as a gambler and
racketeer*) This beautiful structure—(*Gesturing toward the
structure behind him*)—bears the name of a young man who
several years ago received a mortal injury in that great football
stadium across the Mall. The Tom Stark Memorial Hospital.
Tom Stark—(*On the balcony above, in a spotlight,* TOM STARK
*has appeared. He is a handsome, strong, sullen-faced boy, wear-
ing a football uniform, and carrying his helmet. He stands
there, impassive, until just before the appearance of* JACK
BURDEN)—who was he? And why should this hospital be
named for him? He was an All-American quarterback, one of

the finest athletes this state—no, the entire South—has ever produced. Tom Stark's father, as Governor of this state—

MAN

(*Rising from the audience*)
Say it! Can't you even say his name? Damn it—it was Willie Stark!

PROFESSOR

Yes—well, yes—Willie Stark. As Governor of this state, he projected the institution which today we dedicate.

MAN

He was a crook! He built the hospital to fight impeachment!
(*The Governor has risen and is making gestures toward the rear of the audience. The* MAN *is seized and ejected, as the* PROFESSOR *continues.*)

PROFESSOR

He was, let us admit, a controversial figure. But let us not dwell on that. What matters is that the hospital exists. We must remember that historical evolution concerns itself only with the total society, and that individual names do not matter. The hospital is here. In one sense, and in my belief, the deepest and only important sense, it does not matter how it came to be. It does not matter why Governor Stark—Willie Stark—conceived it—

JACK

(*Rising from the audience, a youngish man, darkly handsome and somewhat saturnine, given to moments of brooding withdrawal*)
Crap.

PROFESSOR

I beg your pardon!

JACK

I beg *your* pardon. But you are talking crap, you know.

PROFESSOR

Who are you?

JACK

Burden. Jack Burden. And may I again remark that you are talking crap?

PROFESSOR

I was merely referring to a verifiable phenomenon—a fact. (*Pointing to the structure behind him*) That hospital is a fact.

JACK

I should like to know the truth behind that fact.

PROFESSOR

Truth? A name for excuses. Or, to use your word—crap. That—(*Indicating the hospital*)—is a fact. It does not matter who observes it. It does not matter how it came to be. It doesn't matter why it was conceived—whether as a political expedient to fight an impeachment or as a—

JACK

Stark conceived it because he owed it to something he was.
    (*He has now come upon the stage, followed by* ANNE STANTON, *his wife.*)

3

PROFESSOR

(*Coming down from the platform, approaching* JACK)
Excuse me, Mr. Burden. I must impress upon you that it does
not matter what he was.

JACK

If Stark hadn't been what he was, that hospital wouldn't
exist at all.

PROFESSOR

What if he was a starry-eyed idealist? Or what if, on the other
hand, he was, as he appeared to be by ordinary standards, a
cheap demagogue, a ruffian, hag-ridden by vanity, a drunkard—
but, no, I don't want to allow my personal feelings to intrude,
for as I've already said, in the long view those things do not
matter, the hospital is what—

LUCY

(*Appearing at stage left, a woman of middle age, handsome
in a spare, countrified way, with feeling and dignity, now making a gesture of anguished protest*)
Oh, but Willie wasn't like that!

JACK

Yes, ask Lucy—ask his wife if it matters what Willie Stark
was!

ADAM

(*Appearing at stage right, an intense, finely grained man of
JACK's age, speaking directly to the audience, out of a painful
urgency*)
It mattered that my best hope was fouled—

4

JACK

Yes, ask Dr. Adam Stanton!

ADAM

I did what I did because he breathed the air I breathed. Because he—

ANNE

(*Leaving* JACK'S *side, and moving in protest toward* ADAM)
Oh, Adam, no—don't say it!

JACK

Yes, ask her, Prof—ask Adam's sister, my wife—ask Anne.

IRWIN

(*Appearing near* ADAM. *He is a man of some sixty-five or seventy years, dignified, handsome, well dressed in a severe fashion*)
Ask me.

JACK

(*Taking a step toward him, lifting his hand in excited greeting*)
Judge—Judge Irwin!

IRWIN

(*Ignoring* JACK, *addressing the* PROFESSOR)
Yes, ask me, for the dead have a long time to think. Stark was—

SUGAR-BOY

(*Appearing at stage left, a runty Irish youth, nondescript in*

5

*dress, a shoulder holster visible under his left arm. He speaks
with a stutter, made worse by his present excitement*)
The B-B-B-Big B-B-Boss—he was the Big B-B-B-Boss.

JACK

Ask Sugar-Boy!— Ask Sadie Burke! (*The light is up on
a youngish woman with a pocked face, dark burning eyes, and
a vital intensity*) Ask Tiny Duffy—that bag of guts yonder—
(*Pointing to* TINY, *who, angry, confused and defensive, comes
down from the platform*)—ask him if it matters what Stark
was—(*Waving his arm in an inclusive gesture*)—yes, ask
them all!
    (*As all draw closer toward the* PROFESSOR, *babbling for
    an instant, impelled by a communal need to define them-
    selves and their old relations to* STARK, *the* PROFESSOR *lifts
    his hand, and they are suddenly still.*)

PROFESSOR

What could their sick compulsions mean? Nothing more
than your own, Mr. Burden—mere froth, shall we say, on the
stream of history. What Willie Stark was—(*With irony*)—now
really, Mr. Burden.

STARK

(*Picked out in a spotlight on the balcony is a powerful man of
about forty-five, somewhat gone to seed, but handsome in a rural
way, untidy, but wearing a good dark suit. He does not look
down at the stage, but out over the audience, speaking almost
as though to himself, in a tone of painful meditation*)
You live in the world and you try to know the truth of the
world. You live, and you try to know the truth that is in you.

PROFESSOR

The truth!

SUGAR-BOY

(*Staring up at* STARK, *raptly*)
It's the B-B-Big B-B-Boss—he c-c-can talk s-s-s-so good!

STARK

The truth is there. But you walk in the darkness of the world.
You walk in the darkness of yourself. The darkness whirls.
And in the sick hour before dawn, you are sick of the world.
You are sick of yourself. And you say, "If only—if only—"

PROFESSOR

My dear Governor, in the texture of reality, there is no "If
only"—no "What might have been." At one time I thought you
understood such matters.
(*The light is down on* STARK.)

JACK

(*With a surge of excitement, interrupting the* PROFESSOR)
Hold it! I'll tell you how that hospital came to be built.

PROFESSOR

All right. Tell me. (*Withdrawing a little to stage left*) If
you can.
(*He retreats further, and leans against a girder. During
the entire play he is always present, watching, from one
point of vantage or another, the course of the action.*)

The Light Dims

7

ACT ONE

ACT ONE

In the central area of the stage, now lighted, JACK *moves back toward the platform. The lectern has been removed; a bench is visible toward the rear.*

JACK

Once upon a time, I was in my mother's house, the big white house a man named Burden had walked out of and left my mother and me—and never said why. He had left my beautiful mother, whom I loved and hated. Who had married all those men after he left her—and tonight—now, now—lies up there behind the jalousies with a taffy-haired bastard named Murrell, nearly ten years younger than she.

(At the clink of glass, he swings back and quickly lies down on the bench, as though sleeping. His MOTHER *enters into the light, a handsome woman of indeterminate years, wearing a robe, carrying a tray with a bottle of whiskey, a siphon, and glasses with drinks already mixed.)*

MOTHER

I heard you moving—I thought I'd bring you a cold drink.

JACK

(Rising)

I heard you, too. I heard the cork pop. I heard the gurgle.

MOTHER

Oh, son, son—don't be like that. I didn't touch it. I just heard you moving around and thought you might have a nightcap. (*Having set down the tray, she offers a drink to him*) A nightcap with me.

JACK

Why don't you have it with that beautiful, taffy-headed, new, cretin husband of yours?

MOTHER

He's asleep— Be nice to him, son. Be nice, just a little. You're not nice to anyone here at the Landing any more. You didn't even call Judge Irwin when you got in today, to say hello. (*As he takes the glass and drinks from it*) What's the matter? You're not like you used to be. Not like yourself.

JACK

Before I'll be like I used to be, I'll shoot myself.

MOTHER

And Judge Irwin was like a father to you when you were a boy. Didn't you have a good time with him, son? When he took you hunting? When he taught you how to sail? When he—

JACK

Oh, cut it out!

MOTHER

(*Sitting down, drawing him down beside her, then making him lie with his head in her lap, his glass still in his hand*)
Listen, don't leave in the morning. I'm having dinner with Judge Irwin tomorrow. Stay, son—he'd adore it. You like the Judge, don't you?

JACK

(*Jerking himself away, rising*)

Like I like booze!

(*He drinks.*)

MOTHER

He loves you, son. (*The phone rings and she answers*) Hello. (*She covers the mouthpiece, turning to* JACK) It's those people! Those voices. You can always tell those voices. Why don't you stay here? You belong here. You don't belong with that kind of people—that scum off the human pot, that canai—

JACK

(*Mimicking, picking up the phrase out of old familiarity*)

—that scum off the human pot, that canaille—but, oh, they love me. (*Seizing the phone*) Hi, Boss.

(*The light comes up on* SADIE, *stage left.*)

SADIE

(*Speaking into the phone*)

Listen, you patrician poop. Hell has popped. MacMurfee's boys in the Legislature are starting impeachment proceedings to-morrow. On the Boss.

JACK

Has MacMurfee got anything?

SADIE

It doesn't matter what he's got. It matters how many bastards he's bought. Or scared.

JACK

Well, the Boss wasn't born yesterday.

SADIE

Oh, he's playing rough. The boys are out and they're dragging in the sore-tails and wobblies in the Legislature. Lot of 'em here right now, weeping and praying. They are strictly crying for Mother. The Boss has something on most of 'em.

JACK

Don't tell me the Boss would use any of those undated resignations.

SADIE

Shut up, Educated, and listen. The Boss is coming down there. Now.

JACK

To the Landing? Here? What the Christ-sake for?

SADIE

Plenty. One of your high-toned pals down there—Judge Irwin —has knifed the Boss.

JACK

He has?

SADIE

Endorsed the impeachment.

JACK

For God's sake.

SADIE

Yeah, it's a fact. In the morning paper tomorrow. We got a leak.

JACK

What do I do?

SADIE

Be standing out in front of Judge Irwin's house in half an hour.

JACK

Okay. And then what?
> (*As the light goes down on* SADIE, JACK *stands with the phone in his hand, staring at it. There is a repeated offstage echo, "And then what?" over and over, like the rhythm of anesthesia, fading. As* JACK *stands there, the* PROFESSOR *approaches, from a point of vantage.*)

PROFESSOR

Don't you remember, Mr. Burden? You took Stark to your old friend Irwin in the middle of the night. Stark and his little stuttering pathological gunman.

JACK

Sugar-Boy wasn't a gunman. He was just a little Irish runt that had bad teeth from sucking cube sugar, and that got kicked around and never had a dime till the Boss found him.

PROFESSOR

And made him his gunman.

JACK

Oh, he could shoot. I won't deny that.

PROFESSOR

Or deny that you took them—him and Stark—to Irwin in the middle of the night.

JACK

No, I don't deny it. Sure, I was reluctant to take Stark to
Irwin. I had been happy there with Irwin, years back. I had
been happy at Burden's Landing with Adam Stanton and his
little sister Anne. —Anne Stanton, oh, she was the night and
day, and she sang to me of what innocence and love I have
known.

ANNE

(ANNE *appears at stage right, in a girlish dress.* ADAM *is near her,*
further forward, in a tennis rig, with a racket, looking toward
the audience. Throughout the following, the characters are not
speaking to each other, but forward toward the audience)

I was happy there once. I saw the moon rise over the sea, and
I was happy. There were Adam and Jack and I, and life was a
bright promise. Life was a promise, and—

JACK

(*With a gesture forward, as though calling*)

I'll race you to the raft!

ANNE

(*Facing forward*)

I'll race you!

(*There is a sound of laughter, offstage, and the splash.*)

ADAM

(*Facing forward*)

The net, Anne—cover the net!

REFEREE'S VOICE

(*Offstage*)

The games are now four-all.

ADAM

(*Still speaking forward*)
Atta girl, Anne—oh, that was a beauty!

JACK

(*Still speaking forward*)
You are my beauty, dear Anne—oh, Anne, see the moon come
over the water—

ANNE

(*In her own dream, with a cradling gesture of her arms, singing*)
Oh, Jackie-Boy—oh, Jackie-Bird—sweet Jackie-Boy—

JACK

(*Singing*)
Oh, darling Anne, see the moon rise over the water—

ANNE

But the water gets cold, it is cold, and the moon goes down,
and life drives them past, flat and fast over the net, and life
drives them past you and you see them coming but oh, it is
gone, flat and fast over the net—

REFEREE'S VOICE

Game and set. It is game and set.

ANNE

And life slips through your fingers like wind. It leaves you—
and what you dream leaves you. Those whom you love leave
you. They withdraw from you and you are alone.
(*The lights are down on* ANNE *and* ADAM.)

17

JACK

And it is all flown away.

PROFESSOR

(*Moving into the area of light*)

So there you are, waiting in the middle of the night.

(*There are the lights of an approaching car, the sound of brakes and the slam of the car door.* STARK *enters from the shadow at stage left, wearing a light topcoat, fawn-colored, and a homburg. He seems gay and confident.* JACK *turns toward him in alarm.*)

JACK

Hey, Boss—what—

STARK

Easy boy, it had to come. And now, by God, it's here! I've got 'em out of the brush, I got 'em out in the open now, and I'll ride 'em down!

SUGAR-BOY

R-R-R-Ride 'em down, Boss! Ride 'em d-d-d-down!

STARK

(*Mussing* SUGAR's *hair with an affectionate gesture; turning to*

JACK)

By God, they'll remember this day. MacMurfee—Mac-Murfee—his unborn great-grandchildren will wet their pants on this anniversary and not know why. It will be the sins of the father and wet pants unto the tenth generation.

JACK

Judge Irwin—what are you going to say to him?

18

STARK

(*Gaily*)

You never know till you look 'em in the eye. I just want to look him in the eye.

JACK

Look here, Boss—the Judge won't scare.

STARK

I just want to look him in the eye.

JACK

God damn it, the Judge won't scare.

STARK

Let's get him out, Jack. (*As* JACK *hesitates*) Get the bastard out.

(*As* JACK *moves toward stage left, the light is up on* IRWIN, *seated under a desk lamp, reading. There is a bust of Thomas Jefferson, on a plinth, profile to the audience. As* JACK *enters,* IRWIN *rises cordially, placing a hand on* JACK's *shoulder.*)

IRWIN

Well, Jack—Jack my boy! Come in. What can I do for you? (*As* JACK *seems disturbed, unable to speak*) You're not in any—in any—trouble?

JACK

No, Judge, I'm not in any—

STARK

(*Suddenly stepping into the light of the* JUDGE's *study*)

No, Judge, Jack's not in any trouble. Nor me. (*As* IRWIN *seems taken aback*) Ain't you asking me in, Judge?

IRWIN

I beg your pardon, I was about to retire.

STARK

Not yet, Judge.

IRWIN

(*As* STARK *pushes past him, followed by* SUGAR-BOY)
You—you even bring your—your bodyguard.

STARK

Hell, Judge, Sugar's just a pal.

IRWIN

If you think the presence of a hired gunman can intimidate
me—

STARK

Hell, Judge, Sugar wouldn't hurt a fly. He's just a pal. A pal
that drives my car for me. Ain't you my pal, Sugar?

SUGAR

Sh-sh-sh- sure, I'm j-j-j-just a—

STARK

Swallow it, Sugar.

IRWIN

If you have any business, make it brief.

STARK

(*Discovering a tray with a bottle and glasses*)
Judge, the best business I got on my mind is what's in that
bottle there. I trust you don't mind if Jack pours me a slug.

IRWIN

I did not realize, Jack, that your duties include those of a body servant. But of course, if I'm mistaken—

STARK

Nuts, Judge. Sometimes Jack pours me a slug and sometimes I pour Jack a slug. And sometimes I pour myself a slug—(*Pouring a drink, then sitting in the* JUDGE's *chair*)—whether I'm asked or not. For I am a very impatient man, Judge, and there are a lot of things you never get if you wait till you are asked. That is why I am not what you would term a gentleman, Judge.

IRWIN

Really?

STARK

Yeah, but you—you're a gentleman, Judge. Is that why you endorsed my impeachment?

IRWIN

I owe you no explanation.

STARK

Oh, you said this state needed better roads and decent schools and an income tax. I did those things. By God, I did 'em!

IRWIN

You accomplished certain necessary reforms, but the Supreme Court of this state ruled—

STARK

—that my income tax was illegal, that my extraction tax was illegal. They ruled it. But the court reversed itself, didn't it?

IRWIN

After you had packed the court.

STARK

Hell, all courts are packed from the start. It just came my turn to pack it.

IRWIN

You have flouted the Constitution, you have flouted the rule of law—

STARK

You know, Judge, the trouble with you is, you're a lawyer. You're a damned fine Harvard Law School lawyer.

IRWIN

You're a lawyer, and you ought—

STARK

Hold it, I'm not your kind of lawyer. Oh, I know me some law. Fact is, I know me a lot of law, even if I never went to any silk-hat law school. I can see what the law is like. The law is like a single-bed blanket on a double bed and three folks in bed on a cold night. There ain't ever enough blanket to cover the case, and somebody is always nigh to catch pneumonia. Hell, the law is like the pants you bought last year for a growing boy, but it is always this year and the seams are popped and the shank bones to the breeze. The law is always too short or too tight for growing humankind. And that, Judge, is why I made me up some law. To protect folks from the kind of law you and your kind make up, and by God—

IRWIN

I do not care to discuss the matter with you.

STARK

You ain't discussing it, Judge. I am. And while I'm at it, I'll just tell you why you want to impeach me.

(*He rises from the chair, facing* IRWIN.)

IRWIN

I followed the dictates of my conscience.

STARK

Which ain't a thing but the conscience of every corporation and bank in this state. Oh, you were a friend to the common man. Oh, you talked about sweet reform until you saw I meant business. Real business. And then something happened inside you, Judge, and you call that something your conscience.

IRWIN

If you mean to imply that I've been dictated to—

STARK

Oh, the silk hats didn't have to buy you, Judge, for you are one of them. And that's why I'm telling you right now that I'm just getting started. And nothing will stop me—nothing—

IRWIN

That is precisely the point. You will stop at nothing. Some of your personal methods have come to my attention.

STARK

Oh, somebody's been digging up some dirt, huh? Some of the sweet-smelling?

IRWIN

If you choose to call it that.

STARK

Now dirt is a funny thing, Judge. (*Going back to the chair, settling himself comfortably*) Come to think of it, there ain't anything but dirt on this green God's globe. It's dirt makes the grass grow. A diamond ain't a thing in the world but a piece of dirt that got awful hot. And God-A-Mighty picked up a handful of dirt and blew on it and made you and me and George Washington and mankind, blessed in faculty and apprehension. It all depends on what you do with dirt, ain't that right, Judge?

IRWIN

The facts are clear. What you say makes no difference.

STARK

No difference, huh? Well, this makes a difference. I can run this state. I'll run it any way I can, and that can make a big difference to you.

IRWIN

I shall take my chances.

STARK

Judge, you ain't got but one chance, and this is the last one. You been sitting back in this fine room, and nigger boys been single-footing in here bringing you toddies, and you been guessing right. Oh, you took a little time off from duck hunting and corporation law to do a hitch as Attorney General. You been playing at being a judge for a long time. How would it feel not to be a judge any more?

IRWIN

No man has ever been able to intimidate me.

STARK

And I'm not trying to, Judge. Not yet. I'm just telling you that you don't know a thing about politics. Not my kind, Judge. I'm just telling you the facts of life.

IRWIN

I'll thank you, sir, to get out of that chair and to get out of this house.

STARK

Jack, you were right. The Judge don't scare easy.

IRWIN

Get out.

STARK

Those old bones don't move so fast, but now I've done my bounden duty, let me rise and go. (*Spying the bust of Jefferson, greeting it like an old friend, slapping it on the shoulder*) Damned if it ain't old Tom Jefferson. Hello, Thomas! (*Studying the face of the bust, his hand still patronizingly on its shoulder, then speaking in the serious tone of a school elocution class*)

"Can storied urn or animated bust
    Back to its mansion call the fleeting breath?
Can Honor's voice provoke the silent dust,
    Or Flatt'ry soothe the dull cold ear—of Death?"

(*Shaking his head, he pats the bust on the shoulder, and turns to* IRWIN)

Well, Judge, more in pain than wrath I go. And if you and your conscience ever see the light—in a reasonable time, of course—

IRWIN

Get out.

STARK

Let's haul ass, Jack.
(*He starts toward the center of the stage.*)

IRWIN

Your employer has called you, Mr. Burden.

JACK

I don't use an ear trumpet yet.

IRWIN

I'm dining with your mother this week. Shall I tell her you
like your work?

JACK

Sure, Judge. You tell her that. But if I were you I wouldn't go
advertising this visit. Someone might think you had stooped to
a low political deal in the middle of the night. With the Boss.

IRWIN

Boss!
(*The light is down on* IRWIN *as* JACK *joins* STARK *at stage
center.*)

STARK

You were right, Jack. The Judge didn't scare. (*Chewing his
cigar meditatively, then taking it from his mouth and twisting
it in his fingers*) But why can't he understand me? Why can't
he, now? You know, there was a time I figgered he understood
me. Damn it, he's just like Lucy.

26

JACK

Lucy?

STARK

Yeah. She might leave me. Separate.

JACK

Sadie—is it Sadie?

STARK

No. She don't know about that.

JACK

Lucy's a woman, isn't she. And they can smell it.
(*He sits on a block, his back to audience.*)

STARK

No, it's not Sadie. It's just that Lucy don't like the way I do
things. Like the Judge, she don't like my methods.

JACK

It looks like everybody is trying to run your business.

STARK

God damn 'em. Damn 'em all. Oh, they like what you do.
They think it's great. But they don't like the way you do it.
They want to spit on you. But there's just one way. And by
God, I know the way.

JACK

And you do things that way.

STARK

Even you.

JACK

I didn't say a word.

STARK

Gimme a slug.

JACK

You know where it lives.

(STARK *lifts* JACK's *coat, takes a flask from his hip pocket, and drinks.*)

STARK

This sure ain't as good as Irwin's. (*Hands* JACK *the flask*) You know—you know what I'm going to do? As soon as I beat this impeachment.

JACK

Sure, take a long rest. Make a novena. Get drunk.

STARK

Nope. I'm going to build me a hospital. I'm going to build the Goddamnedest, biggest, chromium-platedest, formaldehyde-stinkingest free hospital and health center the All-Father ever let live. Boy, I tell you, I'm going to have a cage of canaries in every room that can sing Italian Grand Opera and there ain't going to be a nurse hasn't won a beauty contest at Atlantic City, and every bedpan will be eighteen-carat gold, and, by God, every bedpan will have a Swiss music-box attachment to play "Turkey in the Straw," or the Sextet from *Lucia,* take your choice.

JACK

You'd better bust MacMurfee first.

STARK

Oh, I'll bust him, I'll—(*Angry, as an idea strikes him*) Listen, Jack, you get in there and dig. Get the dirt on the Judge.

JACK

Look here, Boss, there isn't any dirt. Not on the Judge.

STARK

There's always something.

JACK

Maybe not on the Judge.

STARK

Listen, Jack. Man is conceived in sin and born in corruption, and he passeth from the stink of the didie to the stench of the shroud. There is always something.

JACK

But, Boss—the Judge—

STARK

He's a man, ain't he? And if he's a man—
(STARK *turns abruptly and goes.*)

PROFESSOR

(*Moving from the shadows, where he has been watching*)
So, Mr. Burden, in the midst of your "inner struggle," you thought you could have it both ways—that you could dig as Stark commanded, but in the end, prove that Irwin was the man you had always thought. That was terribly unrealistic. But Stark, he was a realist. The hospital proves it. He conceived it to assure the public of his good faith while he was under impeachment. And it was tactically necessary that he do so.

29

JACK

Stark conceived it because he wanted to do something for the people of this state, pure and simple.

PROFESSOR

That is merely a justification. I tell you I am not concerned with justification. I am concerned with the ultimate end, and what that end delivers to society. Not with your sugar-coated justification of the means to that end.

JACK

But the reasons for an action must be justified. For that is what makes a man. If man cannot justify—

PROFESSOR

My dear fellow, can't you see that your whole point of view is irrelevant? All this moralistic moonshine about personal justification. But even in your own deluded terms, what sense are you making? How would you justify Stark when he set out to terrorize a legislature—blackmail, thuggery, conspiracy—he carried his appeals from one end of the state to the other— he inflamed the lawless and illiterate—

JACK

He went to the people and he inflamed them with hope.

PROFESSOR

A blind mob, fed on promises—

JACK

He promised them only their right. They were the ordinary people of this state—the society of this state. If they are worth nothing, then how can this hospital be a "good"? It is for them.

ALL THE KING'S MEN

STARK'S VOICE

(*Offstage, addressing a crowd*)
Your will is my strength.
Your hope is my justification.
Your need is my law.
Your heart is my own.

JACK

(*Moving to stage left to challenge the* PROFESSOR)
What if that were true? Yes, Prof—what if it is true?

PROFESSOR

The hospital is here. It is a "good." No matter if the particular
society it serves is, at the moment, illiterate and decadent. And
that, Mr. Burden, is what you must understand.

TOM

(*In a spotlight, on the platform, wearing his football uniform*)
I tried to understand him and what it was I was supposed to
be. But all that mattered was that I watch the ball arch toward
me through the hot sun and that I take it and cradle it to me
and run for the glory of the Great God Willie. That was what
I had to do in order to be called "Son." Oh, but I tried, I held out
my hand to him and said, "Father, Father, help me, love me."
But he never heard, and so, in the silence, there was nothing left.

LUCY

(*Appearing in a spotlight, stage right*)
But he wanted to know you, Tom. He never meant to—

TOM

Mother, I was your son. Why couldn't that have been enough?

LUCY

Oh, I wish you could have known him as I did. For then you would have known that there was in him something to love.

JACK

(*To the* PROFESSOR, *as the light goes down on* LUCY *and* TOM)
Yes. Lucy knew him, and I knew him too. I'll tell you what he was, back when I first saw him. And if you can understand that, you will understand what you must understand. It was back in 1930, and I was in the back room of Slade's speakeasy with Tiny Duffy, who was city assessor, a city hall swell with a hard straw hat and a diamond ring and lard oozing sweetly from every pore. (JACK *moves to the platform, stage center, where the light comes up on* DUFFY, *reading a paper, in shirt sleeves, on his head a hard straw hat with a garish band. A table with a red-check cloth is before him.* SLADE, *a waiter, is in the background. To* DUFFY) Who's this guy you waiting for?

DUFFY

Name of Stark. From the sticks. Hey, Slade, will you turn that damned thing down? Name of Stark. County Treasurer up in Mason County. Some hick. I never laid eyes on him. A guy's bringing him to me to see about some school bonds they're trying to float up there. Just to get the benefit of my advice, my experience.

MAN

(*Entering, escorting* STARK, *in a tight seersucker coat, loud tie, hair slicked down, full of rural diffidence*)
This is Willie Stark, gents. From up home in Mason City. And this—this is Mr. Duffy. Yes, sir, this is Mr. Duffy. Just like I told you.

STARK

(*Shaking hands*)

Mr. Duffy.

MAN

This is Jack Burden—he's a newspaperman.

STARK

(*Shaking hands scrupulously*)

How'do, Mr. Burden.

JACK

How'do.

MAN

Yeah, Willie here is from up home, at Mason City. Me and Willie went to school together. Yeah, and Willie was a bookworm. He was the teacher's pet. Wasn't you, Willie? And he's still the teacher's pet, damned if he ain't, ain't you, Willie? Willie married a schoolteacher.

DUFFY

(*With ponderous humor*)

Well, they tells me that schoolteachers are made with it in the same place.

MAN

Gawd, Mr. Duffy, you sure are a card! Now ain't Mr. Duffy a card, Willie?

STARK

Yeah, Mr. Duffy is a card.

SLADE

What'll it be, Mr. Duffy?

33

DUFFY

Beer all around.

STARK

Not for me, thank you kindly.

DUFFY

Beer all around.

STARK

Not for me, thank you kindly.

DUFFY

You bring him a beer.

STARK

No, thank you.

MAN

Maybe the schoolteacher don't let him drink nothing.

STARK

Lucy don't favor drinking, for a fact.

DUFFY

Well, what Lucy don't know don't hurt Lucy, does it? Give him a beer.

STARK

No, thanks.

MAN

Maybe she lets him drink orange pop. Hey, Slade, you got any orange pop?

SLADE

I got orange pop for them as wants it.

STARK

I reckon I'll have me a orange drink.

SLADE

(*Giving pop to* STARK)

Pop.

MAN

Yeah, Willie's County Treasurer for two years now up in Mason City. He's getting into politics.

DUFFY

Politics! (*Staring incredulously at* STARK *as he drinks the pop, soberly like a child*) My God.

JACK

(*Moving to stage right as the light goes down on the others*)

"My God," Duffy said, and you couldn't blame him. Willie was in politics, but not for long. The Commissioner wanted to give the school contract to a gentleman who happened to be his brother-in-law and who, by the way, did not offer the lowest bid. But Willie wouldn't sign. So they threw Willie out. He knew they would throw him out and throw out Lucy, who was teaching school, but he didn't sign.

LUCY

(*Appearing on the platform, stage center*)

No, he wouldn't. And one day they had a fire drill at the school. The fire escape pulled loose, because the schoolhouse was built of politics-rotten bricks, and eight poor little scholars hit the concrete walk and were killed. We went to the funeral—the

35

big funeral for all eight of them. We stood in the back, and Willie was just standing there when old Mr. Sandeen saw him and shouted, "It's God's judgment on me for not listening to an honest man. May God bless Willie Stark who tried to save my little Sallie!" And I was proud that he had done what was right, Willie had. And he always wanted to—he wanted to do what was right—you must believe it—you must—

(*The light is down on her, cutting off her urgency.*)

PROFESSOR

(*Moving toward* JACK)

But that accident, it was fortunate, wasn't it, for Willie Stark? For Stark's connection with the accident made one faction of the Democratic Party try to use him in the primary.

JACK

Sure, the Harrison gang wanted a stooge. So Willie was picked for the sucker. I was along covering the campaign, for the *Chronicle,* what there was to cover, with Tiny Duffy, and Sadie Burke, who was one very tough cookie, from up in the Yankee North. Just the night before what was supposed to be the big barbecue and rally, Sadie was sitting in my hotel room, gloomy as a constipated owl. (*The light is up on* SADIE, *as* JACK *takes a chair*) It's no go, Sadie.

SADIE

What's no go?

JACK

You know what I'm talking about. Willie is no go.

SADIE

Maybe he'll pick up.

JACK

Listen, Sadie, that guy couldn't steal a vote from Lincoln in the Cradle of Confederacy. Those speeches.

SADIE

(*Wearily*)

Yeah, ain't it awful?

JACK

Why don't you tell the big boys back in town it's no go? Get the sap out of his misery.

SADIE

What do you mean?

JACK

Come on, Sadie. We are old pals. I won't print it, but I know it's a frame-up. Willie is a dummy candidate to split MacMurfee's cocklebur vote.

SADIE

Look here, now.

JACK

It's a frame-up. Anybody could see that. Anybody, but Willie.

SADIE

Okay. It's a frame-up.

JACK

Why don't you tell the big boys it won't work? Get the guy out of his misery.

SADIE

I told 'em a long time back. I told 'em it wouldn't work. Let 'em spend their money. They wouldn't listen to me.

37

JACK

I'm not worried about their money. It's the sap.

SADIE

You know, suppose they told him. He might go on making those speeches. Even if he found out he was a sucker.

JACK

Maybe.

SADIE

God, aren't they awful?
(STARK, *in shirt sleeves, enters, and hesitates in embarrassment.*)

JACK

Hey, look. It's Willie. Come on in, Willie. Give Willie a drink.

SADIE

He don't take it.

JACK

Oh, yeah. Have a seat, Willie.

STARK

No, thanks, Jack. No, thanks.

JACK

What's on your mind?

STARK

(*Standing aimlessly*)
Nothing. Nothing special.

JACK

Come on, spill it.

38

STARK

It's just—it's just I wondered.

JACK

Wondered what?

STARK

How do you think it's going?

JACK

What's going?

STARK

My campaign.

JACK

Fine. I think it's going fine, Willie.

STARK

They didn't seem to be listening so good yesterday.

JACK

You tell 'em too much. It breaks down their brain cells.

STARK

Looks like they'd want to hear about my road program. And my tax program.

JACK

Just say you're going to soak the rich.

STARK

What this state needs is a balanced tax program. Now, the ratio between income and—

JACK

We heard the speech.

SADIE

(*Speaking to him over her shoulder as she refills her glass*)
Hell, make 'em laugh. Make 'em cry. Stir 'em up. They aren't
alive, most of them and haven't been in twenty years. (*Moving
toward him, warming to the topic*) Hell, their wives have lost
their shape, likker won't set on their stomach, and they've lost
their religion, so it's up to you to stir 'em up. Make 'em feel alive
again. For half an hour. They'll love you for it. Hell, heat 'em up.

STARK

I've heard that kind of talk.

SADIE

It's no secret. It gets around.

STARK

Maybe I can't talk that way.

JACK

That's the only way you'll ever be Governor.

STARK

A man don't have to be Governor. (*Hesitating, gulping*) I'm
not denying I wanted it. I wanted it. A man can lie there at night
and just be so full of wanting something that he just plain for-
gets what it is he wants. Like when you are a boy, and the sap
first rises good in you, and you think you will go crazy some
night just wanting something— Gee, Miss Burke—I apologize—
talking that way before a lady—

SADIE

I ain't a lady.

STARK

I could have made a pretty good Governor, too. By God—by God, better'n Joe Harrison—better'n MacMurfee. I know what people need. You know why? I know because I never had 'em. Look at me—I never had a day's decent schooling in my life. I *know* what people need. I would have made a pretty good Governor—

JACK

Hell, the votes haven't been counted yet.

STARK

No, Jack, I won't make it.

SADIE

If you don't stop talking like that—oh, you make me sick.

STARK

I'm sorry, Miss Burke. But it's just the way I feel. And I'm sorry to be telling you what I'm going to tell you. After you've worked so hard to help me and been so nice. It ain't that I don't appreciate it and all, but—

SADIE

What—what are you trying to say?

STARK

It's just that I'm quitting, Miss Burke. I'm not man enough, and I know it. I'm going back home to Mason City, and farm and practice me a little law. That's all I know how to do.

SADIE

You mean that you're resigning?

STARK

I mean it. I won't ever be Governor.

SADIE

Listen to him! He won't be Governor. Whatever made you think you could be Governor? Look at yourself. (*A vindictive edge coming into her tone*) Whatever made you think it? You were framed. Do you get it? Framed.

STARK

Framed?

SADIE

And how! Oh, you decoy, you dummy, you woodenhead, and you let 'em because you thought you were the little white lamb of God—Baa aa— But you know what you are? You are the goat. The sacrificial goat. Oh, you sap!

STARK

Why did they frame me?

SADIE

Oh, my God. Listen to him. He wants to know why. I'll tell you why. If you can get it through your thick skull. To split MacMurfee's vote in the sticks.

STARK

Jack, is that true?

JACK

That's what they tell me, Willie. (*As* STARK *sits with a stricken look,* SADIE *thrusts her drink into his hands, and he desperately gulps the whole glassful*) Hey, take it easy, you aren't used to that stuff.

SADIE

He ain't used to a lot of things. Are you, Willie? You ain't used to the idea of not being Governor.

STARK

I was used to it. To not being Governor.

SADIE

Well, you better stay used to it.

STARK

I was used to it, but not now.

SADIE

Not what?

STARK

Not used to it now.

SADIE

Not used to it now. My God! He says he's not used to it now.

STARK

(*Rising from his chair, seizing* SADIE *by the shoulders, shaking her*)

I'll kill 'em. I'll kill 'em. I'll—

SADIE

Sit down and shut up.
(*She shoves him so that he falls back into the chair.*)

STARK

I'll kill 'em.

SADIE

Oh, you won't do a Goddamned thing. Not you, you tin-plated, one-gallus sap, you.

JACK

I don't know what kind of games you play. But I'm not going to stay here and watch.
(*He exits.*)

SADIE

(*She fills a tumbler half full of whiskey*)
Take it, you sap. Take it, it's all you got left.

STARK

I'll kill 'em.

SADIE

(*Crouching on the floor before him, a hand on one of his knees, thrusting the glass up at him*)
Take this and shut up, you— Come on, drink it.
(STARK *gulps the drink, as* SADIE, *fascinated, stares at him. He shudders with the drink, then finds her staring up at him, as the light dims out and comes up again on* JACK, *downstage.*)

JACK

I couldn't stay and watch it. So I walked out, and put the town to bed. When I got back Willie was out cold. He didn't look like a winner. The next morning either, when I tried to get him on his feet for the big political barbecue. He was Weary Willie and his face was pale and pure. He couldn't keep a thing on his stomach. Not even water. But I finally tried the hair of the dog, and he had near a pint of whiskey in him by the time I got him to the fair-grounds.

(People—rural types—begin to move around the platform as the entire stage is lit. DUFFY *takes a seat on the platform, fanning himself with his hat. We hear the band playing "Hail, Hail, the Gang's all Here."* STARK *unsteadily mounts the platform.* JACK *and* SADIE *appear stage left.)*

DUFFY

(Rising)

And now, friends, I give you our next Governor. Willie Stark.

STARK

Friends, I have a speech here. It is a speech about what this state needs. But you wouldn't listen to it. And you're right not to listen to it. You are right not to listen, because you already know what you need. Look at your pants. Have they got holes in the knees? Listen to your belly. Does it ever rumble for emptiness? Look at your kids. Are they growing up ignorant as dirt? No, I'm not going to read you any speech. No, folks, I'm going to tell you a story.

JACK

(To SADIE*)*

What's that booger up to?

SADIE

(Engrossed)

Shut up.

STARK

It's a funny story. Get ready to bust out laughing. It's about a hick. A red-neck hick like you.

MAN

Who you calling a hick?

45

STARK

Yeah, you heard me! A red-neck hick like you. He knew what it was to get up before day and slop and feed, with cowdung between his toes, and then walk six miles to a slab-side schoolhouse. He knew about red-clay roads so gully-washed they'd string-halt his mules. Oh, he knew what it was to be a hick—summer or winter.

MAN

Summer *and* winter.

STARK

And he figured he'd have to help himself. For nobody ever helps a hick.

MAN

God's truth!

STARK

So he sat up nights studying law. Not in any man's college, but at night after a hard day in the field. He sweated so he could change things. For himself. I'm not lying to you. He wasn't any Tin Jesus. He was out for number one—himself.

MAN

Every time!

STARK

But something came to him on the way. How he couldn't help himself without helping other hicks. That came to him. And it came to him with the power of God-A-Mighty's own lightning on the day when back in his home county the first brick school ever built there collapsed because it was built with politics-rotten brick and killed eight pore little scholars. Oh, you know what happened, and how he tried to stop it.

MAN

Yeah, he tried.

WOMAN

Willie tried!

STARK

And the big boys in the city knew it, too. So they came riding up in a fine automobile. Up to his Pappy's red-clay farm, and said how they wanted him to run for Governor. Because he was an honest man. Oh, they sweet-talked him. But you know what they wanted, those crooks in the striped pants? What they never told him. They wanted to use that little hick to split the hick vote for MacMurfee and help elect their secret boss, Joe Harrison. Joe Harrison, that deadhead!

MAN

How do you know that?

STARK

(DUFFY *has risen in alarm*)

How do I know? I know because that fine woman right there —(*Pointing to* SADIE)—she told me the truth. The truth that stinks in the nostrils of the Most High!

DUFFY

(*Toward stage right*)

Play the "Star-Spangled Banner"!

STARK

(*Pointing to* DUFFY)

And there he is! The man that fooled that hick. There is the Judas Iscariot, the lick-spittle for Joe Harrison.

DUFFY

(*Desperately*)

Play the Goddamned "Star-Spangled Banner"!

(*As* DUFFY *leans toward the band,* STARK *boots him on the behind so that he falls off the platform.*)

STARK

(*As the crowd starts angrily toward* TINY)

Let the hog lie! Let him lie, and listen to me, you hicks. I'm resigning from this race. In favor of MacMurfee. That's not because I love him. But to beat Joe Harrison. So vote. Vote to beat Harrison. And next time—next time, you hicks—I'm coming back. For I have got me a gospel. Oh, Lord, I've got me a word. Take this state for it is yours! Oh, Lord, I have seen a sign! Oh, Lord, you have given a sign to Gideon! Dew on the ground and the fleece dry! (*The crowd chants, "Gideon, Gideon, and the fleece dry!"*) Oh, Lord, I am coming back and under God's holy hand no man will stop me. I will smite him. Hip and thigh, shinbone and neckbone. Kidney punch, rabbit punch, and solar plexus. For, oh, Lord, I have seen a sign. Blood on the moon! It'll be their blood. Gimme that meat ax. (*Leaning toward the crowd, holding out his hands. The crowd lift up their hands as though passing the ax up to him*) Blood on the moon!

(*The crowd roars.*)

The Light Blacks Out

ACT TWO

ACT TWO

STARK

(*Offstage*)
Your will is my strength.
Your hope is my justification.
Your need is my law.
Your heart is my own.

JACK

(*In the light, stage center*)
In 1938, Willie Stark came back, and it was hell among the
yearlings, and when the smoke cleared away not a picture hung
on the walls. And in the midst of the steaming carnage, there
wasn't anything but Willie.

PROFESSOR

(*Moving toward* JACK)
Oh, yes, there was. There was. There was Sadie Burke. By
that time the Boss's mistress.

JACK

All right, she came along. But she paid her own fare, for she
was a smart fixer. But it was Willie had the gospel. For the
people.

PROFESSOR

And there was you, Mr. Burden—there was you—

JACK

All right. I came. I came because—

PROFESSOR

Because being incapable of action in your own confused and wasted life, you had a romantic admiration for action. Oh, you fancied the role of the cynical observer, but deep inside—

JACK

All right, all right—

PROFESSOR

All right, and there was Duffy. Don't forget him, Mr. Burden, the crook Stark made his Lieutenant Governor.

JACK

Sure, he used him. And if you are the scientific realist you fancy yourself, you ought to know why. Willie had been wised up and knew what he had to do. He had to use Duffy.

PROFESSOR

Oh, I don't object. It was historically necessary to use Duffy. I merely want to keep the record straight.

JACK

Well, to keep the record straight, had you thought of this? That Stark had Duffy because Duffy was another self—the self the Boss could give every insult to and contempt—what one self of Stark did to the other self as a tribute to what Stark wanted to be?

PROFESSOR

That is amateur psychology, Mr. Burden. He wanted Duffy because Duffy was a crook, plain and simple. And it was Duffy who, when Stark was under impeachment, fixed up the rotten contract with Larsen for the hospital, and who—

JACK

That was exactly what Stark did not want. Duffy had tried for a long time to make Stark do it—
> (STARK *is shown at the left, in his office area, seated, with a bottle of pop.* SUGAR-BOY *is at one side, cleaning his revolver.* DUFFY *is standing, leaning toward* STARK. JACK *moves into the scene, waiting.*)

DUFFY

Boss, I got a neat little trick, Boss. It'll sure kill the impeachment. It'll make MacMurfee get down and say "Uncle."

STARK

Spill it, Tiny, spill it.

DUFFY

Well, you know Larsen—Mr. Larsen—

STARK

Sure, I know Gummy. He's a crook. Just like you, Tiny.

DUFFY
(*Grinning feebly*)

Now, Boss, I wouldn't say that. And, Boss—Mr. Larsen, he's a pretty important man, you know. He's got a chunk of the Morton Bridge and Construction Company, he has a—

STARK

He *is* the Morton Bridge and Construction Company.

DUFFY

Well, Boss, I just happened to run into him on the street the other day and we sort of got to talking—

53

STARK

Hey, Tiny, will you get off the pot?

DUFFY

Well, now, you know how it's Mr. Larsen sort of calls the tune for MacMurfee—he puts up the jack—

STARK

Yeah? You don't tell me.

DUFFY

Well, you know he ain't so satisfied with MacMurfee any more, he—

STARK

You mean he wants to sell his pal out?

DUFFY

Now, Boss, I wouldn't put it that way. Mr. Larsen admires you, Boss. He was just saying—how he admires you and—

STARK

Gummy Larsen admires a dollar bill.

DUFFY

Oh, he admires you, Boss. He knows what's going on. He's seen how you got the goods on lots of them guys in the Legislature. He's seen you handling the impeachment, Boss, and he admires you for it. He figures how you and him might work together and he could fix things up all smooth, Boss, no trouble.

STARK

What does he want?

54

DUFFY

Well, you know he's got that fine construction company.
Mighty fine.

STARK

What does he want?

DUFFY

Well, now, that hospital—you know this hospital of yours—

STARK

(*Rising, sadly*)

You know, Tiny, I got to try harder to understand you. I got
to cultivate me an understanding heart, Tiny. And you got to
try to understand me, too.

DUFFY

(*Laying his hand on* STARK's *shoulder*)

Sure, Boss, I understand you. You—you're old Willie—and
you know how all us boys feel about you.

STARK

(*With manly sweetness*)

Yeah, Tiny, I know how you feel.

DUFFY

I know you know, Boss. And, Boss—(*Pawing* STARK's *shoulder*)—this business with Larsen would be slick—(*Delighted with himself*)—it'll be slick. And, Boss, I got a surprise for you!
(*Gesturing to stage left, rear.* LARSEN *appears, composed and watchful.* STARK *stares at him an instant, dumfounded, as* DUFFY *continues*) Yeah, Boss, I knew you'd want to see Mr. Larsen. I
just knew you'd want to talk a little turkey with Mr. Larsen, I
knew—

STARK

(*Moving on* DUFFY, *but speaking in a low, grating, controlled voice*)

Say it again, and I'll strangle you. Larsen won't touch my hospital—Larsen or nobody like him. And you—you hyena-headed, feist-faced, belly-dragging son of a slack-gutted she-wolf—(*With an anguished look at* LARSEN, DUFFY *flees.* STARK *turns on* LARSEN) And as for you, Gummy—

(LARSEN, *completely calm and cold, confronts him, rolling a cigarette between a thumb and forefinger.*)

LARSEN

My dear Governor, it is all a matter of timing. The timing was bad. It seems you aren't ready to do business with me. (*He turns calmly to go, then looks back over his shoulder at* STARK) But you will, Governor.

(*Before* STARK *can collect himself,* LARSEN *is gone, leaving* STARK *to swallow his rage.*)

STARK

That Duffy—that Tiny—if he thinks he can—(*Turning to* JACK) You know what Lincoln said?

JACK

What?

STARK

He said a house divided against itself cannot stand. Well, he was wrong. This house is standing, and it's half slave and half son-of-a-bitch.

JACK

Yeah—and which is which?

56

STARK

Slaves down in the Legislature, and sons-of-bitches up here. (STARK *sits at the desk, brooding a moment*) Damn it, nobody understands me, not even you. (*After a pause*) I'm gonna build the biggest and best hospital money can buy. And any man or woman or child, in sickness or in pain, can walk through those doors, and know that all man can do will be done to cure sickness and ease pain. Free. Not as a charity, but as a right. And I don't care if he votes for me or not. You hear me? (*Rising, with a sudden idea*) Adam Stanton—Dr. Stanton—he is one of your high-toned pals, isn't he?

JACK

He's my friend.

STARK

I want him.

JACK

What for?

STARK

The hospital—what else would I want him for? I want him to be the director. He's the best. I want the best.

JACK

You'd better take the Keeley cure. He hates your guts.

STARK

I don't care what he hates. I want him.

JACK

You are dreaming dreams.

57

STARK

I dream lots of dreams. But, by God, I can make 'em walk. Get him.

(*As* STARK *withdraws, the* PROFESSOR *approaches*.)

PROFESSOR

So you believed Stark, and tried to deliver your friend over to him.

JACK

Why shouldn't I have believed him?

PROFESSOR

Ha, ha. If you want reasons, which one of a dozen would you like to hear?

JACK

All right, all right. (*The light comes up on* ADAM *in his office, stage right; an x-ray plate is in his hands.* JACK *enters the office. To* ADAM) Still don't lock your door?

ADAM

Well, Jack! Gee, I'm glad to see you.

JACK

I'm sorry to bust in on you when you're so busy and—

ADAM

Never too busy for you, boy. What's on your mind?

JACK

Well, Adam, Stark wants you to be the director of that hospital he's planning.

ADAM

Jack, you know what I think of Stark. You know me.

JACK

Oh, sure, Stark is a tough baby. Sure, he plays rough, but this thing—why, this hospital is going to be the nuts—the biggest thing ever. Why, I've heard you say a thousand times that what this state needed was a decent health program—hospitals—clinics—and, boy—

ADAM

It will be an instrument for power—a tool for graft.

JACK

Not this time. Why, this thing is his baby. Any crook tries to lay a finger on it, and he'll tear him limb from limb. And—he expects you to write your own ticket.

ADAM

Did you come here to buy me? Does Willie Stark think he can buy me?

JACK

He knows he couldn't buy you, Adam.

ADAM

Or threaten me? That would be next.

JACK

No, he couldn't scare you.

ADAM

That's what he seems to depend on. The bribe or the threat.

JACK

Guess again.

ADAM

Well, I'll not be flattered by—

JACK

By any man, Adam. Oh, no—you're too proud for that. For you *are* proud, aren't you, Adam?

ADAM

I'm too proud to be any man's tool, and if that is pride—

JACK

Not a bribe, not a threat, not flattery—guess again.

ADAM

What are you driving at?

JACK

He knows your little secret.

ADAM

You go back and tell your boss that I've got no "little secret."

JACK

He knows your little secret—and I'll tell you what it is.

ADAM

What?

JACK

You want to do good. (*As* ADAM *turns away in confusion*) Well, it's no disgrace. It may be eccentric, but it's no disgrace. You want to heal the sick. And the Boss—he—

60

ADAM

I told you I'll do nothing for him.

JACK

But, Adam, a ten-million-dollar hospital, every facility you have ever dreamed of. We know you're respected, but aside from that, what have you got now? A one-horse practice in a small town, and a batch of research papers that might get read some-day. You take that directorship and people will listen.

ADAM

I told you I will do nothing for him.

JACK

Not even good?

ADAM

Good—that's a hell of a word to use around him—the Boss!

JACK

If a thing is good, it is good in itself.

ADAM

A thing does not grow except in its proper climate, and you know what climate Stark creates.

JACK

A good is a good, pal. Is the rose less of a rose for the dung in the ground? Is a love sonnet any worse because the guy who wrote it had hot pants? Is a—

ADAM

You are completely irrelevant.

JACK

That's what you always used to say when we were kids, pal,
and I won the argument. Could a lion whip a tiger? Is Keats
better than Shelley? Is there a God? I always won the argument,
and you always said I was irrelevant— But Little Jackie is never
irrelevant, and I leave you with that thought. 'Bye, Adam. (*Re-
appearing near stage center as the light is down on* ADAM) And
I might have left him alone forever to be whatever he was, to
do what good he could do, sunk in his work and his isolation,
and not have bothered him about the hospital any more. If
Anne had not asked me. But even then I could not have per-
suaded Adam, if when I dug on Judge Irwin I had not found
something I never expected to find. (ANNE *is revealed in a spotlight.* JACK *continues talking as he approaches to take her arm*)
And I had the documents in my pocket as Anne and I walked
the streets that night and came to the docks on the river.

ANNE

All right, Jack, why is he so against it?

JACK

(*Stepping back from her*)

I don't know, I tried.

ANNE

But you can make him do it. You're the only person he loves.

JACK

Anne, it's impossible.

ANNE

Then try harder.

JACK

Listen, Anne, I think the best thing for Adam is to let Adam
alone.

ANNE

Alone, that's the trouble. He's alone—he has withdrawn from me, from us, from the world—and it's killing him and it's killing me.

JACK

Yeah, I know.

ANNE

Please, Jack.

JACK

Anne, it's impossible.

ANNE

I can't believe there's no way to make him.

JACK

There's no way to make him because, to be perfectly brutal, he is the son of Governor Stanton, the grandson of Judge Peyton Stanton, and the great-grandson of General Morgan Stanton. It is because he is a romantic, and has a picture of the world in his head, and when the world doesn't conform in the slightest particular to that picture, he wants to throw the world away. Even if it means throwing out the baby with the bath.

ANNE

Make him do it.

JACK

It means changing the picture in his head. (*With a dawning idea*) It would be like an operation—like cutting a chunk out of what makes Adam Adam.

ANNE

I don't care. I want him to do it.

JACK

How much do you want that?

ANNE

(*Embracing him with sudden lover-like intensity*)
More than anything in the world.

JACK

(*As she releases him*)
Are you sure?

ANNE

Sure.

JACK

Okay. Okay. But I couldn't ever do this if you hadn't asked me.

ANNE

Do what?

JACK

What I am going to do. Damn it, there's only one way.

ANNE

What way?

JACK

By giving him a history lesson. What we students of history always learn is that man is not good or bad, but bad *and* good—

ANNE

Tell me.

64

JACK

—and the good comes out of the bad—and the bad comes out of the good, and—

ANNE

Oh, stop it and tell me.

JACK

Remember, you asked me.

ANNE.

Damn it, Jack. You're just talking so you won't tell me.

JACK

Back in 1928 Judge Irwin was broke. His house and his plantation were mortgaged. But he was State Attorney General.

ANNE

Oh, Jack, I know all that. Back when Father was Governor.

JACK

Yes. Irwin was State Attorney General. The state had a suit against the Southern Belle Coal Corporation. Well, Irwin killed the suit.

ANNE

Irwin—Judge Irwin—took a bribe?

JACK

No greasy bills in a back alley. Just some stock in one corporation to help pay off the mortgage. And a nice job as attorney to take care of the debts.

ANNE

Tell me, what has this got to do with it? With me—with Adam?

65

JACK

(*Coming to put an arm around her shoulders*)

There was a man named Littlepaugh who had been attorney for the corporation that took Irwin. They threw Littlepaugh out to make a place for Irwin. But Littlepaugh raised a kick. And they laughed in his face. So he went to the capital to see your father, and to demand an investigation of Irwin and the Southern Belle—

ANNE

(*As* JACK *withdraws from her*)

Jack, was my father— You *are* a coward! God, you're a coward. You won't tell me. Did they buy him too? Did they, did they?

JACK

It's not that bad.

ANNE

Well, if it's not that bad, then how bad is it?

JACK

Your father threw Littlepaugh out. Unfortunately, Littlepaugh killed himself. Jumped out of a window.

ANNE

Not that bad! (*Collecting herself*) I don't believe it.

JACK

Anne, I don't like it any better than you do. But it's true. I have the proof. Littlepaugh wrote a death letter to his sister. I got it. I have the stock transactions. Oh, I have all the documents.

(*He takes some papers from a pocket.*)

ANNE

(Withdrawing from him, she sits down, leaning forward, sick and weak)

I don't want to see them.

JACK

Anne, I'm sorry.

ANNE

(Numbly)

If you were sorry, why did you get them? *(Jerking up)* Yes, why *did* you get them?

JACK

Damn it—if you must know, I got them for Stark.

ANNE

So you got them for Stark. *(Leaning forward weakly again, laughing, shaking her head at the sad humor)* So that's what it all comes to. So that's what our lives have all come to. You had to go dig it all up. For Stark.

JACK

I didn't want to tell you. But it's the only way.

ANNE

For what?

JACK

To make Adam do what you want—

ANNE

Oh—oh—*(Rising with sudden decision)* Give me those papers!

JACK

What? What are you going to do?

ANNE

Show them to Adam. (*She seizes the papers from his hand*)
Yes, isn't that what Stark would want? Isn't that what you would
want—since Stark would want it?

> (*The light is down on* ANNE, *and, as* JACK *stands listening,
> we hear an echo—offstage—over and over:*
>   *Stark would want*
>   *Stark would want*
>   *Stark would want—*
> *Then the light is down on* JACK.)

ANNE

> (*Reappearing at stage right, the papers no longer in her hand,
> speaking toward the audience*)

No, not for that. Not for Stark. It was to save Adam, to bring
him back to the world—

ADAM

> (*Appearing at stage right, further forward than* ANNE, *with the
> papers in his hand, staring at them*)

And she put them in my hand, and she said—

ANNE

> (*Toward the audience*)

Can't you see you are living a lie? Can't you see you can't
live in the past, for the past was not what you think—

ADAM

And she said—

68

ANNE

Even our father, Adam. Even our father—

ADAM

God damn his soul to hell. (*Pausing, as he stares at the papers*)
They struck me where I was weak. My friend, my sister—

ANNE

Oh, do what good you can—and forget the way it's done—

ADAM

They struck at the point where what I was, was joined to
what the past had been. It was the joint between what good I
dreamed and what good I dreamed the past had been. The
splice was imperfect, the nail was rusted, the solder weak. And
at that point, I broke.

PROFESSOR

(*Approaching from stage left, where he has been watching*)
For all your scientific training, Doctor, you were as romanti-
cally deluded as all the rest.

ADAM

Deluded? My God, he came to my office—even to my office
Stark came!
(JACK *ushers* STARK *and* SUGAR *into* ADAM's *office*.)

JACK

Governor Stark, this is Dr. Stanton. You've already met his
sister, Anne.

STARK

(*Standing solidly before* ANNE, *who is seated, then turning toward* ADAM)
Yes, I've had the pleasure. Nice to meet you, Doc.

ADAM

(*Very reluctantly taking* STARK's *hand*)

How do you do.

STARK

(*Looking down at the clasped hands*)

See, boy, it's not nearly as bad as you thought. It didn't kill you. (*As* ADAM *jerks his hand away,* STARK *turns to* ANNE) It didn't kill you, Miss Stanton, the first time you shook hands with me?

ANNE

Why, no, Governor. Of course not.

ADAM

Won't you be seated?

STARK

Well, Doc, what do you think of it?

ADAM

Of what?

STARK

Of my hospital, boy.

ADAM

I think it will do the people of this state some good. And will get you some votes.

STARK

Forget about the votes, Doc. I don't have to build a hospital to get votes. I know lots of ways to skin a cat.

ADAM

So I understand.

STARK

Yeah, it'll do some good. But not too much good unless you take over. You're the man for it. And Jack here says you've agreed.

ADAM

I won't tolerate any interference.

STARK

Don't worry. I might fire you, boy, but I wouldn't interfere—

ADAM

If that is a threat—

STARK

Boy, I wouldn't threaten you.

ADAM

I believe you know my views of your administration. They are no secret. They will be no secret in the future. Do you understand?

STARK

No offense, Doc, but I could run this state with you howling on every street corner like a pup with a sore tail. All I want is for you to run that hospital and run it right. Do you understand?

ADAM

I understand that you think my name will be useful to you politically.

STARK

You just don't understand politics, Doc. You don't understand what makes the mare go. (*Rising, casual and amiable*)

You're just like a lot of folks. You want certain things that are nice and right. For instance, you want this hospital and you want the bricks, but don't you know that somebody has got to get down in the mud to make 'em? You are just like everybody who loves a big juicy steak but just can't bear to go down to the slaughter house because there are some mean men down there who aren't kind to animals. Maybe it is all right for me to be down in the mud, huh? Or down at the slaughter house. (*Crossing to stand over* ANNE *and speak challengingly down to her*) I mean no offense, Miss Stanton, but do you think it's honorable to want something and not be willing to pay the price for it?

ANNE

Why—why—I don't know—

STARK

Now, if you think that is honorable, just tell your brother here—

ADAM

If you came here for the purpose of—

ANNE

Adam, please.

STARK

(*Gaily*)

Easy, Doc, easy. It's just that folks like you think you can inherit everything. Just because you inherited your father's name, his brains, and a little money, you think you can inherit everything. But there's one thing you can't inherit. And do you know what that is?

ADAM

No, what?

STARK

Goodness, Doc. Just plain, simple goodness. You want it, but you can't inherit it. You've got to make it out of badness. And do you know why?

ADAM

Why?

STARK

Because there's nothing else to make it out of. Did you know that, Doc?

ADAM

What are you trying to convince me of?

STARK

Nothing. I'm just telling you the facts of life.

ADAM

You don't have to tell me anything. I said I'd take your job. That's all. I'll take the job. And my reasons are my own.

STARK

Yeah, your reasons are your own. But I just thought you'd want to know something about mine.

ADAM

I'm not interested.

STARK

Not even if we're going to do business together?

ADAM

I'm going to run the hospital. If you call that doing business together.

STARK

Doc, just don't worry. You don't have to get mixed up in my business. I'll keep your little mitts clean. I'll put you in that beautiful ten-million-dollar hospital, and wrap you in cellophane, untouched by human hands. But look at my hands, Doc. (*Cheerfully holding his hands out*) Pitch-black. But don't you worry. I'll take care of you, Doc.

ADAM

I can take care of myself.

STARK

Sure you can, Doc. (*With a sudden change of tone, dignified and businesslike*) You will no doubt want to see all the plans that have been drawn up. We have the most reputable architects in the state. Mr. Todd, of Todd and Waters, will call on you. Start picking your staff. It is your baby. Jack'll stay and fill you in on some of the details. (*Suddenly slapping* ADAM *on the shoulder*) You're a great boy, Doc. And don't let them tell you different. (*Turning to* ANNE) May I drop you somewhere, Miss Stanton?

ANNE

Why, yes— Thank you, Governor.
(ANNE *rises and precedes* STARK's *exit from the office.* ADAM *and* JACK *stare at her, and then, as the light begins to dim, their eyes meet. Meanwhile, the light comes up on* SUGAR-BOY, *who is near center stage, waiting as* ANNE *crosses slowly, followed by* STARK. *He makes a gesture of dismissal to* SUGAR, *who disappears; there is the sound of a car starting and driving off.* ANNE *is standing with her back to* STARK, *some distance from him.*)

74

STARK

Miss Stanton—Miss Stanton—(*She does not turn*) Do you think it's honorable to want something and not be willing to pay the price?

(STARK *steps forward and lays a hand on her shoulder and she stiffens, as the light is down. In the office area, the light comes up on* ADAM.)

ADAM

(*Toward the audience*)

He laid his hand on me, and smiled. "You're a great boy," he said. I was weak. But I came to see. I saw. I saw. And I—

PROFESSOR

(*Approaching*)

And what you saw, or thought you saw, made you perform the final romantic act. For you could not understand the nature of things. You repudiated the world which you could not understand. It proves that what you would call your ideal had no reference to reality, but was, as your sister said, only a self-indulgent dream.

ADAM

I should have struck him where he stood.

JACK

You would have if you had known. You would have done it, for you are Adam. But you didn't know. And neither did I. But I—

(JACK *moves across to stage left, and occupies himself, leaning over the desk, as* SADIE *bursts in.*)

SADIE

The son-of-a-bitch, I'll kill him.

JACK

You having woman trouble with him again?

SADIE

I'll kill him, I swear it. After what I did for him. After I made him. After I took him when he was the Sap of the Year and put him in the Big Time. He can't two-time me, he—

JACK

Look here, my pet, he can't be two-timing you. He was two-timing Lucy with you. Whatever he's doing to you ain't two-timing—it may be four-timing. It may be six-timing. Your arithmetic—

SADIE

I'll kill him. He can't chuck me. Not after I made him. And every time he sees some tart with a pretty face—(*Prodding her face*) Look, look at my face—is it so bad?

JACK

Look here, Sadie, it's not worth the grief. You know him, he—

SADIE

Look at my face—look at it, Jack—did the smallpox make it so bad? And he—

JACK

Come on, Sadie, it's a swell face. Forget about him, forget . . .
(*He tries to comfort her.*)

SADIE

Don't touch me, don't touch me. For it's all your fault. Your

fault, do you hear? You had to bring your high-toned friends—
oh, I didn't mind those common tarts, he always came back, he
came back—but your high-toned friends—oh, it's all your fault!

JACK

What the hell are you talking about?

SADIE

You know what I'm talking about, you pimp. If you were a
man you'd go in there and knock him down. I thought she was
yours. Or maybe he's fixing you up, too.

JACK

What are you saying?

SADIE

Maybe he's fixed you up like he fixed that doctor—that Stanton. Oh, yeah—maybe he'll make you the director of a hospital
to keep you quiet.

JACK

Are you implying that—that—that she—

SADIE

Implying—implying—I'm telling you. That Stanton girl—
that high-toned whore—that whore!

JACK
(*Putting the heel of his right hand to his brow, with a low,
painful utterance*)

Oh—oh.

PROFESSOR

So, unable to face that fact, you got in a car and drove blind
for two thousand miles to Long Beach, California.

JACK

But the past rode with me all the way. It followed me like a flood. For I loved her. I loved her.

ANNE

(*Appearing at stage center, facing him*)
You loved me, yes. But you were lost in the world, and so was I. And the years were lost, like sand in the fingers, or wind. For I had needed someone to say, "See, this is the way." (*Holding out her hands*) But you did not.

JACK

Anne, I remembered.

ANNE

And I remember, too. I was eighteen. It was back at Burden's Landing. (JACK *moves forward to take her in his arms. They sink to the platform*) Jack what are you doing? Let me go! No, Jack, no!

JACK

Don't you love me any more?

ANNE

Oh, Jack, you know I love you—I'll always love you— Just you.

JACK

All right. If you love me—now, now.

ANNE

No—Jack—no.

78

JACK

You would have, last week. You almost did. If my mother hadn't come back that night you would have—wouldn't you?

ANNE

It's true. I almost did.

JACK

All right.

ANNE

But, Jack—it's horrible to say, Jack—but I'm glad I didn't.

JACK

I knew it. You don't love me now.

ANNE

I love you. I'll always love you. I love you more than the world. For you are the world—the whole green, beautiful world—you are the whole world—Jackie-Boy. You're older than the world.

JACK

Don't you call me Jackie-Boy. Not after what you said. That you were glad you didn't. That night with me.

ANNE

Don't you understand? Can't you understand? I do love you. I want you. But—

JACK

But what?

ANNE

Oh, don't you understand?

JACK

Damn it, I'm not trying to steal your virginity. If that's what's on your mind. I've tried to make you marry me a dozen times. Right now, will you marry me? Tonight? Tomorrow?

ANNE

Oh, Jack, I love you. And I feel sometimes I might just kiss you and hold you tight and close my eyes and jump off a cliff with you. Or like the time we dived down deep, deep, and kissed in the water. Don't you remember, Jack?

JACK

But now, what about now?

ANNE

I love you now, but it's different.

JACK

How, different?

ANNE

Jack, you don't understand that love isn't like jumping off a cliff. Or getting drowned. It's—oh, it's trying to live, Jack.

JACK

Money—if it's money—I'll get a job. But not with any of these rich bastards here at the Landing. Or through them. Not even Irwin. If it's money you want—

ANNE

You idiot, you silly Jackie-Boy. It's not money and you know it. I'd love you and live in a shack with you and eat red beans, if you'd only understand. If you only knew what you wanted, if you only—

JACK

I want you.

ANNE

That isn't enough. It isn't enough, darling. You've got to want —oh, I don't know how to say it, but you've got to want to live, to live in the world, to do something—something that means something. Oh, Jack—it's just the way you are, you don't want anything.

JACK

(*Jerking away as the light is down on* ANNE)
God damn it. God damn it all.

PROFESSOR

(*Moving into view*)
So, Mr. Burden, you left her. Alone to face the world. Although you knew Stark was the opposite of everything she had been brought up to esteem, still he was the opposite of you. For he could act. He was sure of himself. So when Sadie Burke, somewhat indelicately, informed you of the fact, you, unable to face that fact, ran away.

JACK

Oh, the past rode with me all the way, to Long Beach, California, and it lay with me when I lay naked, at night, on my hotel bed. And lying there, I thought that nothing mattered, nothing, and then I had a vision of bodies, and naked, detached limbs heaving and bleeding from inexhaustible wounds. And that was my picture of the world.

PROFESSOR

You should have hunted up a good psychiatrist.

JACK

No, I didn't need one. For, suddenly, it was funny. For I saw
that even that vision didn't matter. For everything in the world
was only the dark heave of blood and the twitch of nerve, like
the twitch of the nerve in the dead frog's leg in the experiment,
when you run the electric current through it. And I laughed, I
laughed out loud, for if that is true, then everything is like everything else, and it does not matter what happens to anybody—not
to Anne Stanton, or Willie Stark, or Jack Burden. And there is
no God but the Great Twitch. (*Approaching the* PROFESSOR) You
see, back then I was like you. I worshiped the Great Twitch.
Which is the God of your age.

PROFESSOR

I suppose that what you are trying to say is that you somewhat
tardily recognized the physical basis of life.

JACK

Oh, I recognized it, and it made everything look like everything else.

PROFESSOR

But can't you see, that was sentimental, too? For Nature pre-
scribes her own values. Adjustment, balance, health—a sound
mind in a sound body—a well-organized society—a—

JACK

Oh, I know your line, pal, and since I used to agree with it, I
came back. I came back to Willie Stark. Oh, he was well adjusted. He was on top of the world. He had Anne. He had the
opposition licked. It looked as if the hospital was going to be
built his own way. And to top it all, Tom Stark, his son, was a
hero. All-American quarterback—and the crowd roared! Oh, the

Boss was crazy about that boy. The crummy little cock-of-the-walk. Not yet hurt by the likker and the girls.

LUCY

(*Appearing stage right*)
He was a good boy. If they had let him be. But they gave him a ball and they cheered and their spittle was on him— Oh, I did what I could.

JACK

Yeah, Lucy was separated from the Boss, and Tom was the Boss's boy. But she tried. Like the time Tom got in a brawl in a roadhouse, a fight over a girl, and got thrown in the jug, and it hits the papers. Lucy went to see Stark at the Mansion.
(JACK *and the* PROFESSOR *withdraw as* STARK *is revealed brooding alone in his office.* LUCY *enters to surprise him, with a newspaper in her hand.*)

STARK

Lucy! What are you doing here?

LUCY

It's about Tom. It's in the papers. You've got to put a stop to it.

STARK

If you mean stop playing football, I told you—

LUCY

It's not just football. That's bad enough, thinking he's a hero, that there's nothing else in the world—but it's what he has become—he's wild and selfish and idle—and last night, last night, Willie, he was in jail—our boy, Willie—in jail—

83

STARK

No son of mine is going to be a sissy.

LUCY

If you won't think of him, think of yourself—what a thing like this means to you, what—

STARK

I can take care of myself.

LUCY

You will ruin him.

STARK

Ruin him, ruin him! Hell, let him have some fun growing up. I never had any fun when I was a kid.

LUCY

I'd rather see him dead at my feet than what your vanity will make him.

STARK

Don't be a damned fool, Lucy.

LUCY

Oh, Willie, you loved me once—and he's our son—our son.

STARK

Our son—*our* son? I tell you, he's *my* son. *Mine,* do you hear?

LUCY

Oh, Willie—Willie—
(*She turns away, stricken. Suddenly appalled by his own words,* STARK *approaches her, trying to explain to her—to explain to himself.*)

STARK

Listen, Lucy. You remember my father's house. A house set on a bare hill, on the rock chunks, and the wind beat. I lay there at night, just a boy coming on. It was night and I'd look north across that ice a thousand, five thousand, a million miles. The moon was on the snow. The wind would come riding down under that moon. I'd close my eyes, and it was like that million miles of wind was in me. Something inside me just got so big— (*Dismissing the effort to explain himself, to understand himself*) Oh, you wouldn't understand, you wouldn't understand.

LUCY

Oh, Willie, you think you are one thing, but you're another and different. But I know what you are, what you are, deep inside. I know the very bottom of your heart, what it is, Willie, what you never see any more.

SADIE

(*Entering*)

Oh, excuse me please. Tom's here. Lieutenant Boyd brought him in.

STARK

All right, bring him in.

SADIE

(*Somewhat embarrassed*)

Mrs. Stark, I'm—I'm glad they found him. I mean, I'm glad he's all right.

LUCY

Yes, he's all right. And thank you, Miss Burke. (*As* TOM, *disheveled but cocky, enters*) Tom, Tom, are you all right?

TOM

Mom!—what are you doing here?

LUCY

(*Embracing him*)
Tom, you've got to stop getting into trouble.

STARK

Tommy-Boy!

TOM

Well, Your Highness, I gotta hand it to you. Your little tin-badged highway cop tried to get rough with me. Yeah, he tried, but he didn't.

STARK

I told him to club you over the ear if he had to do it to bring you in.

TOM

Yeah, him and how many more?

STARK

Tom, four days before the Stafford game, and you break training. Miss two days' practice and get boiled.

TOM

Don't worry, Daddy dear, I'll be there Saturday to push over a few for you.
(*He pours a drink.*)

STARK

Get your hands off my likker. Maybe you won't ever push over any more. Not if you break training again. Coach Howes has just about had a bellyful of you, and he—

TOM

He wants the championship, doesn't he?

STARK

Yeah, but he'll bench you anyway. And I'll back him up.

TOM

Oh, yeah?

STARK

Yeah, I don't care how hot you are on the field. I don't care if you're a cross between Pavlova and a locomotive. I don't care if you are Napoleon at Marengo, I'll see you never get your hands on a football again.

TOM

No—no, you won't.

STARK

What do you mean I won't? You know me well enough to know—

TOM

I know you well enough to know that you want the championship worse than Howes ever did. Well enough to know you want me there to shove 'em across for you every Saturday, so you can big-shot it around. (*Seizing a cigar from* STARK's *vest pocket, setting it into a corner of his mouth in a parody of his father*) Yeah, it's my boy did it—it's my boy Tom—

LUCY
(*As* STARK *starts toward the boy*)
Willie! Oh, Tom—Tom—don't—

87

SADIE

(*Entering*)

Jack's here with a Mr. Frey.

STARK

Send 'em up.

LUCY

Come on, Tom, come with me.

JACK

(*Entering*)

I'm sorry, Boss, we'll wait outside.

(LUCY *and* TOM *go out.*)

STARK

Come on in, Jack. It's nothing. Lucy just came to see me about Tom. Say, whoever let that get into the papers? (*Seeing the non-descript man being ushered in by* SUGAR) What does he want?

JACK

I think you'd better talk to him. His name is Frey. Governor, this is Mr. Frey.

FREY

Glad to meet you, Governor.

STARK

You want a drink?

FREY

No thank you. (*Bracing himself, with an effort at camaraderie*) Well, Governor—I am sure sorry about what happened last night. Now, I seen Tom Stark play football, and he is sure

sweet. Yeah, and I made me some money betting on Tom Stark.
Now, you take that Alabam game—

STARK

He was pretty good that day—

FREY

Yeah, and to see a boy like that have any trouble, you know—
like last night.

STARK

Oh, hell, damned fool wouldn't give his name, so they locked
him up. But that's not trouble.

FREY

But it's sort of embarrassing—

STARK

Embarrassing? Who the hell's embarrassed?

FREY

To tell the truth, Governor, yeah, to tell the truth—I'm sort of
embarrassed.

STARK

What's the matter? Aren't your pants buttoned?

FREY

Ha-ha. But serious, Governor—it's sort of embarrassing—you
know. It's sort of embarrassing to my little girl—my—Sibyl.
(*He hands* STARK *a newspaper*.)

STARK

This Sibyl—this Sibyl Frey here— Hey, your name is Frey,
isn't it?

FREY

Yeah, yeah, it's my girl. My girl Sibyl out with your boy. Got her name in the paper. It's sort of embarrassing—her name—

STARK

Congratulations, buddy, lots of girls would like to get their name in the paper with Tom Stark.

FREY

Well, Sibyl don't like it. Sibyl is sort of shy. What you might call timid—and she—

STARK

What is this, a shake-down?

FREY

Why, no Governor, it ain't no shake-down. It ain't just what's in the paper, Governor—it's something else—Sibyl—now she—

STARK

Mr. Frey, would you stop gargling and talk?

FREY

Sibyl—she's—she's in a family way.

STARK

Oh, she's so Goddamned shy she's in a family way. Well, what am I, an obstetrician? What the hell do you want me to do?

FREY

It's—it's—Tom. Tom Stark done it.

STARK

Why, you little bastard. It *is* a shake-down.

FREY

No—no, sir—Governor—it ain't no shake-down—no, sir. I'm a father—I mean, Sibyl is my little girl—she's done give her all.

STARK

All her what, Mr. Frey?

FREY

Give her all, like they say.

STARK

(*Putting his arm on* FREY's *shoulder, walking him out*)
Well, Mr. Frey, my advice to you is to go home and tell Sibyl her all is not worth six bits.

FREY

Six bits, six bits! It ain't the money, it ain't. It's my Sibyl—I'm her father—and she's going to have a baby—and if Tom Stark don't marry her—

STARK

(*Jerking from* FREY, *dumfounded*)
Marry! Jack, did he say "marry"? (*To* FREY) Listen. I don't care if your little Sibyl is as full of squaw-fruit as a possum is of grease. I don't care where she caught the disease. Or how. But I'm telling you if you think some six-bit little tart can—

FREY

Tart! Tart! Sibyl ain't no tart. Ask anybody in Duboisville. Ain't no man can say it, Governor or not—

STARK

(*Seizing* FREY)

You'd better thank God I'm Governor. If I wasn't Governor I'd jerk your damned yellow bilious tongue out and wrap it around your neck. I'd cut your heart out and feed it to the hogs. Now get out. (FREY, *protesting all the way, is seized by* SUGAR *and hustled out*) God damn it. They can't do it to Tom.

JACK

Maybe Tom did knock her up.

STARK

Hell, it's a frame-up. You can look in that guy's eyes and see it. (*An idea dawning*) Duboisville. Who else is from Duboisville?

JACK

MacMurfee.

STARK

Sure, and he knows he's losing the impeachment. It's the bastard's last try.

JACK

Looks like your little boy has fixed you good.

STARK

Hell, he's just a boy.

JACK

Boy or not, he's given MacMurfee some ammunition. Well, there's always Tiny's friend Larsen. You can always deal with Larsen.

STARK

No, by God. Deal with Larsen and he'll ask for the hospital contract. And he won't get that, by God. (*A long pause, grappling with the problem*) Jack, you remember I told you to dig on your old pal Judge Irwin?

JACK

Yeah.

STARK

Did you find the dead cat?

JACK

Yeah—what are you going to do with it?

STARK

What do you think? Put the screws on Irwin. Make him beat some sense into MacMurfee's head. MacMurfee will have to listen to him. He hasn't got many friends left. And Irwin's the biggest leg in the stool. Gimme the pussy cat.

JACK

Not yet.

STARK

What do you mean, not yet?

JACK

I mean not yet. I made a promise.

STARK

A promise to who?

JACK

To myself. Not to do anything till I saw Judge Irwin.

STARK

Hell, you go down and ask your old pal is he guilty, and sure, he'll say he is washed in the Blood of the Lamb. But he is washed in whitewash. Gimme the pussy cat.

JACK

Not yet, Boss.

STARK

What the hell do you think I'm paying you for?

JACK

Okay. I quit.

STARK

You mean it, don't you, Jack?

JACK

I mean it.

STARK

Play it your way. But take it from me—he's washed in whitewash.

(*As* STARK *turns away into the darkness* JACK *moves toward stage right, where* IRWIN *is revealed in his study, reading.* JACK *enters.*)

IRWIN

Damned glad you came by, Boy. It's a long time, isn't it?

JACK

Yes, sir, it's been a long time.

IRWIN

Let me fix you a drink—a little gin and tonic never hurt anyone—not you and me at least—we're indestructible, you and me,
aren't we, Boy?

JACK

No, thanks, Judge, no drink, please.

IRWIN

Well, I'm not going to drink by myself. I'll get my stimulation
from your conversation. What's on your mind?

JACK

Well, uh—nothing much.

IRWIN

There is always something.

JACK

Yes, there is always something.

IRWIN

Out with it.

JACK

You don't like Stark's methods.

IRWIN

Oh, let's not talk politics, Jack.

JACK

Let me tell you about your pal MacMurfee's methods. Miss Sibyl Frey, a little tart over in Duboisville, is knocked up, and puts the finger on Tom Stark. It's a frame-up.

IRWIN

What's this got to do with—

JACK

I know it's a frame-up, because MacMurfee offers to fix it up and call off the impeachment if Stark will make a deal.

IRWIN

That can't be true!

JACK

It's true. He wants to make a deal for the Governorship behind your back. Now, is this pretty?

IRWIN

No.

JACK

Well, you can stop it. MacMurfee will listen to you. Tell him he can't be Governor, but our organization will absorb him. Might even let him go to Congress. If he calls off Frey. Will you do it?

IRWIN

Of course not. My God, they're blackguards. Stark and Mac-Murfee. They're all blackguards! I won't mix in that sort of thing.

JACK

Listen, Judge, you've got to. I'm begging you, Judge.

IRWIN

No.

JACK

Judge, please. I'm not kidding.

IRWIN

Jack, I know my own mind. That's about the only thing I've learned out of life. That I know when I know my own mind.

JACK

Well, you decide tomorrow. I'll be back tomorrow.

IRWIN

I've decided tonight.

JACK

Did you ever hear of a man named Mortimer L. Littlepaugh?

IRWIN

No, I don't think so.

JACK

Did you ever hear of the American Electric Power Company?

IRWIN

Naturally, I was their counsel for ten years.

JACK

Do you remember how you got that job?

97

IRWIN

Yes, it was through a man named—

JACK

Judge, change your mind. Judge, I'm begging you. Judge, I'm begging you.

IRWIN

No. I told you no. (JACK *flings the documents to the desk.* IRWIN *reads, then speaks, marveling*) Littlepaugh—Littlepaugh. You know, I didn't even remember his name. I swear, I didn't even remember his name. (*Touching the papers*) It was like this never happened. Not to me. Maybe to somebody else, but not to me.

JACK

But it did.

IRWIN

Yes, Jack, it did. But it is difficult for me to believe.

JACK

It is for me, too.

IRWIN

According to these documents, my dear old friend, Governor Stanton, impaired his honor to protect me. He never told me. His failing was a defect of his virtue. The virtue of his affection for a friend.

JACK

Judge, if that's meant for me—I tell you—

IRWIN

My boy, I didn't mean that—from my heart I didn't. I just wanted you to know about Governor Stanton. That you might think well of him. (*Pause, and then a shift of tone*) I suppose your employer is trying to put the pressure on me? To blackmail me?

JACK

Pressure is a prettier word.

IRWIN

I don't care much about pretty words any more. You live with words a long time. (*Again a shift of tone, to matter-of-factness*) Well, your employer's an attorney, and he ought to know that this stuff won't stick in a court of law.

JACK

Judge, you don't live in a court. You live in the world, and people think you are a certain kind of man. You don't want them to think different, Judge.

IRWIN

By God, they've no right to think different! By God, I've done my duty, I've done what's right—

JACK
(*Indicating the documents*)

Judge—

IRWIN

Yes, I did this, too.

JACK

Yes, you did.

IRWIN

Does Stark know it?

JACK

No. I wanted you to confirm it first.

IRWIN

You have a tender sensibility for a blackmailer.

JACK

You are trying to protect a blackmailer—MacMurfee.

IRWIN

Maybe I'm trying to protect—maybe I'm trying to protect myself.

JACK

Well, you know how to do that then. By stopping MacMurfee.

IRWIN

Jack, I could do it easier than that.

JACK

How?

IRWIN

(*Coming to* JACK, *taking him by the shoulders*)
I could just—I could just say to you—I could just tell you something—something you don't know.

JACK

What? Tell me what?

IRWIN

(*Gaily, withdrawing*)

Nothing.

JACK

Tell me what, Judge?

IRWIN

Nothing. Not a damned thing. Jack—(*Turning away, listening*) You can hear the sea. There isn't any wind, but you can hear the sea rippling on the sand out there in the night. There's a half-moon, and by now it's westering across the water.

JACK

Judge, I'll be back tomorrow. You decide—tomorrow.

IRWIN

Sure, Boy, sure.
(JACK *withdraws, and,* IRWIN, *looking after him, lifts a hand in a gesture of farewell, or benediction, as the light goes down on him.*)

JACK

(*Moving to stage center*)

He had not scared. The Judge had not scared. I walked through the hot night to lie on my bed in my mother's house, and then came the scream.
(*His* MOTHER *appears, stage center rear, with a phone in her hand. She drops it, and screams. He seizes her and tries to stop her hysterics. Then she turns on him.*)

MOTHER

You did it! You did it!

JACK

Did what?

MOTHER

You killed him, you killed him. Oh, I don't know how you did
it—or why—but you did it—you killed him. It was you. Oh, I
know it was you—you—you—you—

JACK

Shut up, Mother. Shut up.

MOTHER

You killed him!

JACK

Killed who?

MOTHER

Judge Irwin—your father—and you killed him!
(JACK *jerks from her, appalled. In a desperate gesture, he
presses a clenched fist against his forehead, and there is the
punctuation of a muted drum-ruffle, offstage.*)

The Light Blacks Out

ACT THREE

ACT THREE

The light comes up on JACK *and his* MOTHER. *They are stand-ing in the same locations as at the end of Act Two.* JACK *is look-ing toward the audience. His* MOTHER *is seated, with her eyes fixed on him.*

JACK
(*Speaking toward the audience*)
So I stood here at Burden's Landing, where I had had, and lost, two fathers. A man named Burden, who had crept away somewhere to rot. And a man named Monty Irwin, who could have stopped me with four short words—"You are my son." Monty Irwin.

MOTHER
And you must love him. For remember, son, I loved him. But love is so small in the wide world. It lies in the palm of your hand like quicksilver, but it slips, it is gone, and the million glittering globules are lost. Or it is the ring you drop in the woodpath, precious and bright and small, and the leaves cover it over. You cannot find it. But, son, remember, I loved him.

JACK
(*Still facing forward, as the light is down on his* MOTHER)
I will remember. I will remember as I walk in the world.

STARK
(*His voice is heard from the dark at stage left, before the light is up on him*)

Jack! Jackie! Jack! (*As light goes up and* JACK *approaches*) So the bastard crawled out on me!

JACK

He's dead. He shot himself. If that's crawling out.

STARK

I didn't tell you to scare him to death.

JACK

(*Approaching with an air of furious assault*)
All you're worried about is your Goddamned hospital. Yeah, that's all! But that's fixed. Yeah, Irwin fixed you good! (*Crowding in on* STARK, *his forefinger threatening him*) And there's only one thing left for you—only one thing left to turn to. You've got to go to Larsen! You've got to deal with Larsen!
(*As* STARK *is driven out of his office, as it were,* JACK *turns and bursts into savage laughter, which is interrupted by football music from the radio on the desk. As* JACK *turns to it, the sports announcer begins.*)

ANNOUNCER'S VOICE

This may be a black day for State—trailing Stafford at the half —but they still have spirit. The band is moving out to spell out that "S"—"S" for State. That's the school they love—listen— (*Band music.*)

DUFFY

(*Enters, escorting* LARSEN)
Mr. Larsen, this is Jack Burden. (JACK *is cold and perfunctory*) You got my word to tell Willie Mr. Larsen might get in this afternoon? You told him?

JACK

Yep.

DUFFY

He ain't here. His office is locked.

JACK

This is a football game. This is for the championship. This is important.

DUFFY

And Mr. Larsen here is a pretty important man, Jack.

JACK

The Boss said to be at the Mansion tonight. Eight P.M. *After* dinner.

DUFFY

Mr. Larsen, would you care to have a seat, make yourself comfortable? (*As* LARSEN *sits,* DUFFY *turns back to* JACK, *pettishly*) Mr. Larsen here is a mighty important man. Great God! Keeping Mr. Larsen waiting for a durn ball game. Looks like Stark would be here now. Looks like he—

JACK

Maybe he does wish he were here. He did not calculate on trailing Stafford University by ten points at the half. He did not calculate on the Sophomore Thunderbolt being back-broke from night life. He did not calculate on the Sophomore Thunderbolt having lead in his pants.

ANNOUNCER'S VOICE

Governor Stark is coming out of the locker room. He has been encouraging his team. With his entourage he is now moving up the sidelines to his box. (*Sound of catcalls, booing and jeers*) This is without precedent! The Governor is being booed!

The Governor is being booed, right in that stadium that he built 'em. Well, I tell you, if I was Governor and I got booed in my own stadium, I would sure be here to see Mr. Larsen. If I was under impeachment, I would sure—

(*Calmly*)
He will come, Mr. Duffy. He is in difficulties.

It is the kickoff— State receives on the twenty— It is Stark— It is Tom Stark—that old Number Two— He is loose—no—no—down on the forty-five—the Stafford forty-five. There's the snap —Yes—yes—it is Stark! Old Tom is carrying the ball—it is the comeback trail—it is the old-time Tom Stark— He's loose—it is a touchdown. No—no—it is not a touchdown—four feet to go— Tom Stark was hurt on the play—Tom Stark is still down. Here comes the doctor on the field. Here is the stretcher. It appears that Tom Stark has regained consciousness.

Well, why don't he leave that little bastard, and come and do business?

But here's the snap—it is a touchdown! These boys will not be denied. It was a straight power play. Pure power. They just boiled over the goal line. Listen to the cheers, cheers for Tom Stark. The Governor has left his box, presumably to go to his son's side.

DUFFY

Well, why don't he come on?

LARSEN

(*Calmly*)

He will come, Mr. Duffy. He is under impeachment. There is even some comment to the effect that Judge Irwin did not commit suicide.

JACK

Look here—Gummy—

DUFFY

Gum— You mean Mr. Larsen, Jack.

JACK

Hell, no, I mean *Gummy,* and I will instruct Gummy that I was there.

LARSEN

Yes. I heard you were there.

JACK

Yes, by God, I was, and—(JACK *swings away, turning to speak over his shoulder*) Stark will see you at the Mansion at eight. After dinner. (*Moving to stage center, as the light is down on* DUFFY *and* LARSEN) Yeah, he would see Gummy Larsen. But before that he had seen his son in the hospital, with a lot of expensive medical talent spooking around the bed. Oh, yes, and the expensive medical talent said that Tom Stark—the Sophomore Thunderbolt—would be all right. Nothing really wrong, Governor. Oh, yes, Governor, we can assure you of that. So nothing was really wrong, nothing really could go wrong for Willie Stark. And the Governor was back to discharge his official function, and I came to the Mansion and it was a real party. The gang was all there.

(*The light comes up on the group, and* JACK *moves to join it.*)

STARK

(*Drinking but not yet drunk, disheveled and bitter*)

Just in time, Jackie-Boy, just in time. Mr. Larsen here is going to build the hospital for me. Tell him, Tiny, tell Jack how puking smart you feel. Tell him how Larsen is going to give you a cut for being so nice—

DUFFY

Now, Boss, that ain't the way Mr. Larsen and I—

STARK

Shut up! You're getting a rake-off and you know it.

DUFFY

Boss, I—

STARK

Shut up. Yeah, look at him. Mr. Larsen used to be a faro dealer, but now he's a big, big-time contractor. And he's just sold out his pal MacMurfee, sold him out to me. Look at that pillar of rectitude, and puke.

LARSEN

If we have arranged our business, Governor—

STARK

Oh, it's arranged, by God. But listen to me, you crook, if—

DUFFY

Boss, don't talk that way to Mr. Larsen. Mr. Larsen is a— (STARK *flings the glass of whiskey in his face, and* DUFFY *moves threateningly, then sees that* SUGAR *has his revolver half out of the holster*) Boss—Boss, what made you go and do that now?

STARK

I ought to done it long ago. I ought to done it long ago. (STARK *turns to* LARSEN, *seizing his lapel*) Yeah, it's arranged, but you— you leave one window latch off, you leave one piece of iron out of that concrete, you chip one piece of marble, and, by God—I'll rip you open—for that hospital's mine. Do you hear? Mine. Now get out.

(*With perfect calm* LARSEN *smiles ironically at* STARK, *and withdraws, followed by* DUFFY.)

JACK

Glad I got here for the last act. Was it fun? Well, I'll leave these papers and toddle.

STARK

Wait. (*Taking a drink from the bottle, weaving on his feet*) I told him. I told him. I said if you leave off one window latch, if you leave one iron out of that concrete, if you—

JACK

Yeah, I heard that.

STARK

I told him, I'll—I'll rip you. I told him. I said—

JACK

So you said.

STARK

I'll rip him anyway, by God! I'll do it anyway. (*With a cry of rage and pain*) They made me do it. They made me do it!

JACK

Tom Stark had something to do with it.

STARK

He's just a boy. He's just a boy. (*He sways*) He didn't mean to. He didn't know.
(*He collapses on the floor.*)

SUGAR-BOY

(*Taking off his coat to spread it on* STARK)
M-M-M-Might catch c-c-cold, Jack.

JACK

Yeah, he might. (*Swinging to the* PROFESSOR, *who has been watching from stage right*)Well, do you think the Boss was a scientific realist that night?

PROFESSOR

He made what arrangements were necessary. But I am not interested in the vaporings around that fact.

JACK

Well, the vaporings are the facts, and the reason—

PROFESSOR

The reason doesn't matter.

(*A telephone, stage left, rings, and* JACK *moves to answer it as the* PROFESSOR *withdraws.*)

JACK

Jack Burden. No, I can't disturb him. Is it important? Well, let me speak to Dr. Stanton. Adam? Yes, it's Jack. What the hell's the matter?

ADAM

(*Appearing in his office, stage right, talking into the telephone*) It's Tom Stark. I'm afraid it's very serious.

JACK

But he was all right a few hours ago.

ADAM

But he isn't all right now. They've just called me in on the case. You'd better get Stark and his wife here right away.

JACK

All right, as soon as I can. (*He hangs up. The light is down on* ADAM. JACK *turns to* SUGAR) Sugar, we've got to get the Boss up and around.

SUGAR-BOY

B-B-ut J-J-Jack, he's s-s-sleeping.

JACK

But this is important. Call Sadie and tell her to bring Lucy to the hospital right away. Then bring the car around front.

SUGAR-BOY

Is it T-T-Tom?

JACK

Yeah, it's Tom, now hurry up.

SUGAR-BOY

You want I should g-g-get c-c-coffee for the B-B-Boss?

JACK

Yeah, Sugar, that's a good idea. That's a fine idea. (*The light is down on* SUGAR *and* STARK *as* JACK *moves forward toward stage left and addresses the audience*) And Tom Stark lay in the hospital that night with Dr. Stanton, the big brain surgeon, brooding over him. The Boss and I had been there a long time when Lucy arrived—and we all had a jolly little reunion in the hospital waiting room.

(*Moving to join* STARK, *seated stage right.*)

LUCY
(*Entering*)

How is he?

STARK

He's all right. You understand?

LUCY

How is he?

STARK

I told you. I told you, he's going to be all right.

LUCY

That's what you say. But what do the doctors say?

STARK

You wanted it this way. You said you'd rather see him dead at your feet. You wanted it. But he—he'll fool you. He's all right. He'll fool you.

LUCY

God grant it.

STARK

Grant it, grant it. That boy's tough. Tough, do you hear?

ADAM

(*Entering*)

He is still unconscious, and paralyzed. The reflexes are totally gone. The x-ray shows us a dislocation of the fifth and sixth cervical vertebrae.

STARK

Where is that?

ADAM

(*Touching the back of his own neck*)

Right back here.

STARK

What are you going to do?

ADAM

The decision will have to be yours. We can put the patient in traction and wait for some resolution, or we can resort to surgery.

This is a technical decision. Therefore, I want you to understand it as clearly as possible. The x-ray can show the condition of the bone, but not of the spinal cord. We can learn that only by operating. If the cord is merely pressed on we can relieve the pressure, and restore some, possibly all, of the function. If the cord is not crushed. If the cord *is* crushed, the patient will remain paralyzed. Do you understand?

STARK

Yes.

ADAM

I must emphasize one other condition. The operation is very near the brain. It may be fatal. It is a radical step. It is an outside chance. It is radical.

STARK

Do it. By God, do it!
(LUCY *nods*)

ADAM

I had assumed that you would make that decision. I've made all the arrangements already.

STARK

He'll be all right, do you hear?

JACK

Sure, Boss, sure.

VOICE

(*Offstage*)
There is a call for Mr. Burden. There is a call for Mr. Burden.

JACK

(*As the light is down on others*)

Anne called me at the hospital. She wanted to know. I told her. "My God, my God," she said. But God wasn't on the other end of the phone. Only Jack Burden, and he couldn't do a thing. And neither could Adam Stanton, that big Doc. For Tom Stark died.

(STARK *and* LUCY *appear at stage center, apart, he staring off into space, she seated and speaking to him across a distance.*)

LUCY

He said Tom was an ideal. A fine, clean ideal for all the boys in this state. Didn't he say that, Willie? Didn't the preacher say that? An ideal. An ideal for all the years to come. Didn't he say that about Tom? (*With a burst of pain*) And it's lies! All lies! Everything is lies, and I can't bear it. The world is lies, and my baby is dead. (*As* STARK *moves to her*) Don't touch me.

STARK

Lucy, I don't know what happened, or how. But I know it happened a long time back, and in darkness. (*Pause*) I want to come back to you, Lucy. (*Pause*) You loved me once.

LUCY

(*Rising, moving away, not facing him*)

I don't deny it. I loved you. But what was once possible is not now possible, at least not now—for I have been in the dark alone, and the dark ticked like a watch, and I remember you laughed and said he was your son, *not* mine—*not* mine.

STARK

He's our son, Lucy. He's our son. (*As an idea comes to him*) I'll tell you what I'm going to do. I'm going to name my new

117

hospital after him. It'll be the *Tom Stark Memorial Hospital and Medical Center*. It'll be—

LUCY

That's what it'll be, and the sports page and the pulpit will do what they do. But, Willie, can't you see? Can't you see those things don't matter? Your name in the papers. Having people cheer. Can't you see? Oh, you'll do it, you'll name it for him, and you can have your son and use him the way you use everybody—but you cannot have my son! Where is my son? Where is he? And it's raining. It's raining on the ground!

STARK

Lucy, I loved you. I love you.

LUCY

If you had loved me you would have made things different. Not the way they are—all ruined when you touch them—whereever you put your hand—

STARK

(*Shutting his eyes as though to shut the world out, and reaching a hand toward her*)

Oh, Lucy—give me your hand.

LUCY

Wherever you put your hand, it was ruin—

STARK

Lucy, give me your hand.

LUCY

If I could understand now—if it were not dark—

STARK

Oh, Lucy, give me your hand.

LUCY

(*A tentative movement toward him*)
If I could only believe—

STARK

(*As her hand touches his, he swings toward her, drops to his
knees before her, flings his arms around her waist*)
Oh, Lucy, I have horrors in my head. They lurch and grind,
like street cars.

LUCY

(*Touching his hair, looking off into the distance*)
He was a good baby when he was little. He never cried.

JACK

(*Turning to the* PROFESSOR, *as the light is down on the others*)
Make what you will of that, pal.

PROFESSOR

What I make of that is simply—

JACK

Wait—and see what you make of this. Next morning, in the
Boss's office—
(JACK *moves to stage left and busies himself at the desk;*
SADIE *sits, glumly smoking.*)

DUFFY

(*Entering*)
Ain't here yet, huh?

JACK

He's coming.

DUFFY

Well, maybe he won't let it get him down.

SADIE

It's just his boy died.

DUFFY

Yeah—tough. (*Pausing ruminatively*) But you know, the Boss ain't what he used to be. Naw, he just ain't got the juice, you might say. (*Edging toward the chair at the desk—*STARK's *chair—and slipping into it*) Mr. Larsen now—I tell you, he is one sharp one. Easy to work with, too. Yeah, let me tell you—

SADIE

You know whose chair you're sitting in?

DUFFY

Huh?

SADIE

So you think it's the Boss that's dead, huh? (STARK, *wearing a hat and top coat, has appeared behind* DUFFY) Well, look over your shoulder and you'll find you're wrong.
(DUFFY *looks around, sees* STARK, *and gets out of the chair as rapidly as possible, cringing as* STARK *hands him his hat, then takes off his coat and flings it over* DUFFY's *arm.*)

DUFFY

Good morning, Boss. How you feel, Boss? We all just came in to see how you feel. Wanted you to know we was thinking

about you. Like everybody in the state, Boss. Look at the telegrams there on the desk. Must be a thousand. Telegrams of
sympathy and condolence. Folks love you, Boss. Yeah, and
flowers at the funeral, they go to show. Them flowers from the
Fifth Ward—that was a real floral tribute, Boss—

STARK

(*Ignoring* DUFFY, *stepping to the desk, giving the telegrams a
contemptuous flick*)

Sadie, get rid of this garbage. (*As* DUFFY *starts out*) Tiny, you
wait. (*Back to* SADIE) Call a special session of the Legislature.
Get together all the stuff you have on Larsen's Construction
Company, and on the Acme Electric. Anything you can on
him, from my private file, and—

DUFFY

Boss—Boss—what?

STARK

You heard me.

DUFFY

Boss—you can't. Boss, you—

STARK

The hell I can't.

(STARK *gestures to* SADIE, *who goes out to follow his in-
structions.*)

DUFFY

Boss, not when everything is fixed with Larsen, Boss, he—

STARK

I can unfix it.

DUFFY

Boss, you can't change your mind. It wouldn't be fair. Not to Mr. Larsen, to change—

STARK

I can change a lot of things around here.

DUFFY

Boss, you call a special session, you start an investigation, you get Mr. Larsen all mad, there ain't no tellin what'll—

STARK

Look here. Larsen may think, or you may think, that he's bought up some of my boys. Oh, I know he's tried. He may give 'em fifty bucks, but I'll give 'em galloping paralysis. They get gay and there'll be a bear market on barbers and farmhands next election, for if there's anything cheap in this state, it's sweet potatoes and statesmen. They both grow on pore ground. And as for you—

DUFFY

Boss, Boss—

STARK

—you may be wearing a hundred-dollar suit and a diamond ring, but on the hoof, you're crow-bait and, boy, I can strip you to the blast. Now get out.

JACK

(*Watching* TINY's *exit*)

Well, you sure like to do things the hard way.

STARK

Okay. I do 'em the hard way.

JACK

I thought you had dealt with Larsen.

STARK

I have undealt.

JACK

It's none of my business. It doesn't matter if you kick Tiny around. He's built for it. But Larsen is a different kind of cookie.

STARK

You've got to start somewhere.

JACK

Start what?

STARK

Skip it, and get me the files on Acme Electric. I'm going to Sadie's office.

(*The light is down on* STARK.)

SADIE

(*Appearing near stage center*)

He came into my office and he told me. He thought he could do it. To me. He thought he could throw me over. Me, who had made him. Sure, he'd fooled around with every little tart in the state, but he always came back. Even that Anne Stanton. He would have even come back from her. But his wife—that Lucy—throwing me over for her! Throwing me over—and trying to shake my hand. Like he was Jesus. Like he was the suffering God.

ANNE

(Near SADIE, *but addressing the audience)*

I understand now, and would not have had it otherwise. I had loved him because I knew what he might have been, and if, in the end, he found what he might have been, why should I complain that that discovery left no place for me? But, oh, it was hard —it was hard—

PROFESSOR

(Moving toward ANNE *as the light is down on* SADIE*)*

My dear madam, even now, when you are satisfactorily married to your early sweetheart, you can scarcely take a rational view of that old event. You had argued yourself by some peculiar, female logic into your liaison with Stark, and then, when he left you, you felt you had lost the only real man in the world. If you had had a little more experience—well, no matter. Sadie Burke, however, had a very different reaction. For when Stark threw her over, she, being a realist, knew exactly what to do.

SADIE

(Appearing at stage left, leaning over DUFFY, *seated)*

Sure, the Boss'll ruin us. He'll ruin you. Larsen will blame you for the hospital contract falling through. And then he'll fix you.

DUFFY

You talking through your hat.

SADIE

You know what the Big Boss has done? He's throwing over that Stanton bag, the whore.

DUFFY

I'll be damned.

SADIE

She may not know it yet, but it's true.

DUFFY

Allow me to be the first to congratulate you—

SADIE

Shut up, you fool. He's going back to his wife.

DUFFY

Sweet Jesus! Haw, haw—

SADIE

Listen. Do you think Dr. Stanton knows the Boss has been rolling Little Sister in the hay?

DUFFY

Sure—don't he?

SADIE

Hell, no, he doesn't know it. Or know that that's why he got that big hospital job. And he doesn't know that the Big Boss is throwing over Little Sister because he—Dr. Stanton—killed his boy, and that's why he's being taken out of that big hospital job.

DUFFY

Is that a fact?

SADIE

Hell, no, you fool. It's not a fact. It's a lie. But Stanton will believe that lie when you tell him.

DUFFY

When I tell him?

SADIE

When you tell him.

DUFFY

Jesus—I couldn't do that, Sadie. If Stanton found that out he might— Well—well, maybe I can get some of my boys to kind of spread the word to Stanton—

SADIE

Sure, put it in the papers, you fool.

DUFFY

But, hell, Sadie, I couldn't tell him—

SADIE

Sure, you're afraid of what will happen when you tell Stanton that he's no better than a pimp. I don't blame you. Not if he's what I think he is—and pray to Christ he is. But then—then— (*Pause*) Then the Big Boss won't do us any more harm, Duffy. And you may escape with your life. And then—

DUFFY

And then, what?

SADIE

And then—(*Drawing wearily away*) Take it or leave it. It's all your funeral anyway.

DUFFY

All right. All right, I'll do it.

SADIE

All right.

DUFFY

Maybe you got something there. Maybe Stanton will fix the Boss. (*Dawning enthusiasm*) Well, I tell you, if me and Larsen take over, Larsen'll sure take care of you. Hell, if we take over I'll take care of you, Sadie.

(*He rubs her shoulders.*)

SADIE

(*With tight lips*)

Get your Goddamned greasy hands off me.

(*The light goes down on the scene and comes up again on* JACK.)

JACK

So Duffy took his life in his hands and told Adam Stanton the big lie. And Adam believed that lie, and I'll tell you why—

ADAM

(*Appearing stage right, toward the audience*)

I'll tell you why. If you have lived in the horrible division of self and yearn for the old integrity. If you have been betrayed by your own father. If you have been betrayed by those you love. If you have lived with the gnawing certainty of self-betrayal. Then you pick each minute like a scab. You wait for the clean twitch of pain. Have you walked a night in the dark, lost on the ground you had thought familiar? And suddenly the lightning flash, the stabbing light on sky, sea and wind-heaved trees, brighter than day—and the old path clear before you. Oh, it is sure. You run in the new dark, while the thunder rolls, and the new dark darker than dark, but it does not matter now, for your feet know. They know the way. At last—and I came to her and saw her face—and would I be the happy pimp? Would I be—

ANNE

(*Suddenly appearing behind and to the right of* ADAM)
No, Adam! Don't you say it. You must understand.

ADAM

(*Turning on her*)
I understand this much. I'll be no front for a scoundrel, or a pimp to your whoring. I'll be no—

ANNE

Oh, Adam, you don't know how it was!

ADAM

I know this much. I know you—(*Pushing her away, so that she falls*) And I know him—and I know his filth. I know his face. And knowing him, at last I know myself.
(*He dashes off as the light is down on* ANNE.)

JACK

(*Appearing in a spotlight*)
And that was their unreconciled parting. Anne called me to find her brother. She said I had to find him. She was wild to find him.
(*The stage blacks out for a moment as we hear* JACK'*s voice and the replies:*
  "*Have you seen Dr. Stanton?*"
  "*No, not all day.*"

"Has Dr. Stanton been here?"

"Hell, no, not today."

"Have you seen Dr. Stanton?"

"No, not tonight."

Meanwhile, the light has come up on ADAM, *stage left, waiting calm and detached, as a* MAN *accosts him.*)

MAN

Howdy, Doc. My God, you been in the Legislature tonight? The Boss is sure on a tear. Maybe they won't get up the nerve to impeach him. He's given 'em heart failure. It's like a hoot owl done got in the hen house. The air is full of feathers. God-A-Mighty, the Boss is like a one-legged man tromping out a prairie fire. I'm tellin' you he sure is tearin' that Legislature apart. The things he's calling them. Things I wouldn't even call my own mule. Man, that Legislature is scared to impeach Willie, with that crowd come into town. That crowd would kill 'em if they tried to impeach Willie. (*Roar of the crowd, offstage*) By God, he's out there. He's out there on the balcony! Bet he's talking to the crowd. Man, I'm going to be there.

STARK

(Offstage)

And my enemies say that I have done things not for the love of you, but for the love of power. Do you believe that?

CROWD

(Offstage)

No! No! No!

STARK

(Offstage)

What man knows the truth of his heart? But I shall look in my heart and hope to find some love for you. Some little at least.

CROWD

(*Offstage*)

Willie! Willie! Willie!

STARK

My enemies say that I have used threats, deals, bribery, corruption. That I have preyed on the weakness of men. Do you believe it?

CROWD

Kill 'em! Kill 'em! Kill 'em!

STARK

What I have done, I have done. And I will not excuse myself. What I shall do I will do. I will do what I must do, but I want one thing. I want to be able in the end to look you in the eye. Listen, listen to me!

CROWD

Blood on the moon! Blood on the moon! Willie! Willie! Willie!

STARK

But listen! Listen! I want that much innocence!

CROWD

Blood on the moon!

ADAM

(*To himself*)

You labor for innocence, and in the end you learn that inno-

cence is easy. It comes as easy and unsought as a childhood recol-
lection. It is as easy as the dearest breath. As the most casual
farewell. As the sea hawk's white highest gleam in the sun. Innocence is easy.

STARK

(*Entering stage right, followed by* SUGAR *and* JACK, *stopped by
several newsmen. There are flashes of camera bulbs as* STARK
stops for picture. Then he sees ADAM *move to him with out-
stretched hand*)
Well, Doc. (ADAM *presents a revolver and fires twice.* STARK
stumbles to his knees, as SUGAR *leaps forward, firing. Even after*
ADAM *is down,* SUGAR, *at a last twitch, fires again.* JACK *is leaning
over* STARK. SUGAR *joins him, as the light is down on the body of*
ADAM) Jack—the Doc—he—he shot me.

JACK

Oh, Boss—Boss—

STARK

Jack, Jack—why did he—do it—to me—

JACK

God damn it, I don't know!

STARK

I never did anything to him—Jack.

JACK

No—no.

STARK

Maybe he just got screwed up.

JACK

Yeah, yeah—he just got screwed up.

STARK

Maybe—I just got myself screwed up.

JACK

Boss—Boss—

STARK

It might have been different, Jack—even yet—even yet—you got to believe that, Jack.

JACK

I do, Boss, I do! I believe it. (*Rising and moving toward the audience, as the light is down on the others*) Different! It might have been different. And I must believe that. (*Swinging to the* PROFESSOR, *who has entered the area of light*) And you—you must believe that. (*To the audience*) For if we believe that, we can live, we can have a reason for living.

PROFESSOR

Mr. Burden. No, no. Those words were only the final indication of Stark's failure of nerve. For in the last phase—after his son's death—Stark became the sentimental, confused moralist, unable to deal with facts. You may think that I have no concern with morality. Oh, but I do. But the morality of an act, the means to an end, must not be confused with the end result. We can only strive to create conditions of health and well-being which will make men well adjusted and therefore able to act morally. Mr. Burden, are you too blind to see that Stark's late conversion to what you regard as a moral view accomplished nothing more than to pass on power to that—to Governor Tiny Duffy!

DUFFY

(*Revealed on the platform, addressing the audience*)
—and friends, after all these years, on this memorable occasion, I can still promise you that Willie Stark's great dream will come true. I have built his hospital. I have kept faith with Willie Stark because I loved him— We all loved Willie—

SADIE

(*Appearing in a spotlight, moving toward* DUFFY, *accusingly*)
Loved him! Loved him. My God! He killed him.
(*She covers her face with her hands.*)

PROFESSOR

And when you found that out, Mr. Burden, what did you do?

JACK

(*Staring at* TINY)
I did nothing. Because he is nothing, nothing. If he were something. If he were real. If he were human. I would have killed him. But he is nothing. He is the Great Twitch. He is the mob in which everything looks like everything else. He is the wind with the stink on it, and we do not know where it comes from. Unless it comes from us. From us all. For if that is the world, that is the world we made. As you say, Prof, History is blind. But Man is not!

PROFESSOR

You are only a man after all, Mr. Burden.

STARK

(*Appearing on the balcony, looking out over the heads of the audience. The other characters are revealed in various places about the stage, looking up at* STARK)

133

I was a man, and I lived in the world of men. And being a man, I did not know what I was. But I yearned toward that definition. And all my deepest labors had no other purpose. But I was a man, among men. I say this not for forgiveness. For I have no need of that now. All I need now is truth.

PROFESSOR

(*Ironically*)

Truth!

STARK

For that is the last ambition.

JACK

(*Challengingly, to the* PROFESSOR)

And from that I'll make my truth.

(*As* ANNE *joins him he puts his arm around her waist and they move toward* ADAM, *with a gesture of loving reconciliation.* IRWIN, *with an expression of warm recognition, makes a motion toward* JACK *and* ANNE.)

LUCY

(*Lifting her arms toward* STARK)

Oh, Willie, Willie!

SUGAR-BOY

It's the B-B-Big B-B-B-Boss. He can t-t-talk so good.

The Light Blacks Out

134